RAISE YOUR GRADE

RAISE YOUR GRADE

THE ULTIMATE REVISION GUIDE FOR GCSE AND A-LEVEL EXAMS

Dr Denise Gossage
May 2014

This edition first published in 2014 by:

Thistle Publishing
36 Great Smith Street
London
SW1P 3BU

ISBN-13: 9781910198216
www.thistlepublishing.co.uk

This book is dedicated to my sister, Sophie, who is about to start her GCSE and A-level journey. Soph, follow the guidance in this book and you will succeed. Fact!

ABOUT THE AUTHOR:
DR DENISE GOSSAGE

My story starts exactly where you are now, taking my GCSEs and A-levels, coming up to exams, wondering how to do my best.

I went to school to collect my results on Results Day. I remember the anxiety and excitement bubbling in the air as pupils piled into the hall. There was a mixture of smiling, crying and screaming as we all ripped open the dreaded brown envelope.

I headed back to my Dad's car where he was waiting nervously and read my results once more. A clean sweep of As and A stars. He went back to work beaming as much as I was.

I aced my GCSEs and A Levels at state school and went on to get a First class degree in Economics & Accounting at Bristol University. I won a scholarship at Oxford University and did a Masters in Economics, scoring the highest exam results in my class. I topped it off for good measure with a PhD in Economics. I landed a job as a jet set Strategy Consultant with a prestigious international consultancy firm. Only one in every 1,000 applicants gets a job like this. Without top exam results, my CV would have headed straight to their recycling bin. I can't say I always dreamt of being a Strategy Consultant. I didn't even know what a Strategy Consultant was until I became one. But the point is this: when the time came to choose my career, my exam results gave me options. That's what good exam results give you – currency for buying yourself some *options.*

I'm extremely proud of my achievements and the truth is, anyone can do it. The reality is I learnt how to work smart and I stuck to a structured revision approach and exam technique that really works. Time and time again I aced my exams and I'm now reaping the benefits. I'm living proof that you don't have to be a genius to ace your exams.

Sam, Michelle, Sophie and YOU

In sixth form, my best friend, Sam was flunking Sociology. Though she grasped the course material, she didn't have a revision strategy and got a U (Ungraded) in her mock exam. With just a few weeks to go until her final exam, she was in a major panic. I helped her put together a revision plan. It took us a couple of hours to do, but changed everything. Instead of another U, she got a B. I can't help wondering what her grade could have been if she had followed a structured revision approach from the start. Years later my sister, Michelle, was taking her GCSEs. I showed her how to revise and helped her soup up her grades in every single subject. Now my other sister Sophie is starting her GCSEs and I've written this book for her.

And for all you students out there who want to give exams your best shot, fulfil your grade potential and zoom your CV straight to the top of the pile.

ACKNOWLEDGMENTS

I would like to thank my panel of A-grade gurus for sharing their wisdom: Benedict Dyer, Beth Sherlock, Daisy Gibbs, Elizabeth Roe, Emily Motto, Emma Brooks, Fred Banerji-Parker, Hannah Bristow, Jeffrey Poon, Julia Megone, Joe Kang, Jonathan Lindfield, Laura Bates, Maria Newsome, Matthew Hilborn, Megan Powell, Miriam Steinmann, Morganne Graves, Neale Roy, Rita Teo, Robert Griffiths, Russell Whitehouse, Susie Archer, Thomas Pollard and Tom Nichols.

A big thank you goes to my fantastic literary agent, Andrew Lownie, for believing in the book. A special thank you goes to my superstar editor, Ros Gray, for her patience, enthusiasm and kick-ass editorial skills. Most of all, I want to thank my wonderful hubby, Ben, for his support, encouragement and advice throughout this marathon project.

CONTENTS

WHY YOU NEED THIS BOOK

How well we do in exams affects so much of our life. The options available to us after school, our career choices, even our self-esteem. Important life-changing things – all determined by a little bunch of vowels and consonants called 'grades'. We spend years dreading them and sometimes, years getting over them. Exams have a lot to answer for.

Revising for exams can be daunting, stressful or just plain old boring, but sadly there's no getting away from it. If you want the grades your ability deserves, you're going to have to knuckle down and revise.

Take heart, because I promise two things:

1. One day, revision will be over. Done with. Gone. And there's nothing – but nothing – as sweet as a summer after exams. Remember that. When older people tell you "This is the time of your life", it's that summer they're talking about. They're not talking about the shining shedload of revision you have to get through first. They've forgotten that bit.

2. Revision always pays off. The Better You Revise, The Better You Will Do. Notice I didn't say 'The *More* You Revise…' That's because it's not just about how *much*

you revise; it's how *smart* you revise. I'll explain. Read the book.

Hang on, you say. I already know how to revise. I've worked my butt off in class. I have a mound of notes. I'll just have a little read through, job done.

You could do that. But don't. Simply reading your notes over and over again is actually one of the least effective ways to revise. Sure, some of it might go in – eventually – but you will be wasting a lot of time and effort. Follow the approach in this book and revise smarter.

"I never need to revise, it all just pops into my head and flows effortlessly out of my pen," said no one. Ever.

We all know at least one smugster who seems to sail through coursework and classwork, collecting A-grade after A-grade. But rest assured when it comes to exams – there's a lot of work going on behind closed doors. If they're self-assured, it's because they're packing some hardcore revision skills – and they know how to use them. And so will you.

So, I hear you cry, if revision skills are soooo important, how come they don't teach it at school? How come there's no Revisionology?

I don't know why schools don't major on revision skills more. How come, given the bewildering range of skills you are taught at school, Revision isn't one of them? Why isn't Exam Technique on every curriculum? I mean, you can quote Shakespeare, calculate an average in three different ways, dissect a frog and order a cheese sandwich in at least one foreign language. But when it comes to Revision skills, you are left to your own devices.

So naturally you turn to the web for help. In Google's annual *Zeitgeist* study, 'how to revise' was the UK's most popular how-to search in 2011. The problem is, there are literally millions of web sites – of varying credibility – offering tidbits of advice – of varying reliability. So the quest for information turns into a time-consuming distraction.

Real-world A-grade advice

To write this book, I wanted to find out what makes high performance revision. I did exceptionally well in my exams. But how? What did I do that was so effective? And anyway, who says my way is the best way? So I tracked down 25 of the world's most successful, not-smug-at-all students. A-grade revision superstars, all of whom have bagged a place at Oxford University with some smokin' exam results. In each in-depth interview, I asked them to share their top tips and tricks for GCSE and A Level success. I grilled them on all aspects of the big R, ranging from "How did you make Revision Notes?" to "How did you deal with revision stress?"

None of them said: "Eh what?"

All of them said: "God yes that was tricky, here's what I did."

Talking to this panel of impressive grade gurus, two things became blindingly obvious:

1. A-grade students don't all revise in exactly the same way.
2. There is a basic formula for success. It's in this book. It's called PUMP: Plan – Understand – Memorise – Practise.

Those students learned it the long way – by trial and error. But with this book in hand, you don't have to.

Science-backed

There's lots of long-beard scientific evidence to support the advice in this book. I read it all so you don't have to – you've got enough to do. I looked at everything science has to say about learning and memory. The approach in this book includes all the study techniques that science has proved most effective. Luckily, my PhD training set me up nicely for the laborious task of reading gazillions of empirical papers and gathering the evidence. Turns out the top scientists agree with the top students; there are some core definable features of effective revision.

Applicable to all subjects

Studying for GCSEs or A-levels is a multitude of tasks. You have different subjects. You need to understand concepts, memorise facts or demonstrate skills. Everyone has their own strengths and weaknesses and a variety of learning preferences. So the question 'how do I revise?' does not have a single answer. But, drawing simultaneously on the scientific evidence and the real-world experience of A-grade students, I've discovered the basic formula for success. I've broken it down to a simple, four-step battle plan that applies to any subject and any level of study.

No need to wing this one

Whether you're a super bright spark sailing through school or a super hard-worker trying to simply keep up, this book doesn't care. Just doesn't care. If your family, teachers and wealthy benefactors are expecting great things from your exam results, this book says forget that. Forget it all.

Raise Your Grade gives students – for the first time – a practical roadmap to guide you to exam revision success. It walks you through the tools and techniques you need to do exactly what it says on the tin. I debunk some popular study myths and lay out the do's and don'ts of effective revision. In isolation, none of the techniques are new. But brought together in the end-to-end, step-by-step PUMP revision framework, approved by science and successful students alike, this book is unique. You will learn more, in less time.

Now's the time to follow the simple, logical, well-researched, four-phase process this book offers: Plan – Understand – Memorise – Practise. Trust the evidence presented from scientists and A-grade students alike. Go with the flow of an end-to-end, step-by-step process. Be handheld by all the experts in this book.

And no grade-boosting guide worth its salt is complete without a word from the examiners. In a crucial section on How to Master your Exam Technique, *Raise Your Grade* includes guidance from real examiners – the very men and women that will be marking your papers.

Raise Your Grade is your comprehensive guide to exam success. Acing exams is a skill you can acquire. In this short book, I'll take you through everything you need to know.

INTRODUCING
THE PUMP REVISION APPROACH

PUMP is the new high-energy, low-calorie, caffeine-free workout for your brain. With PUMP, you'll be honed, toned and ready to go in just four easy steps. Start PUMP today and get the grades you've always dreamed of.

PUMP is a simple framework that takes you through revision from beginning to end. PUMP stands for this:

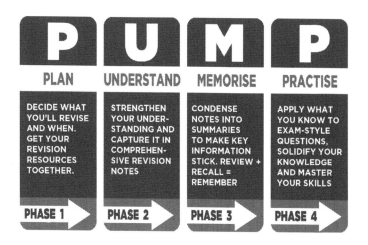

Which basically means...

	YOU'LL BE DOING THIS	YOU'LL BE THINKING THIS
PUMP Phase 1: PLAN	Decide what you'll revise and when. Get your revision resources together.	I'm scarily organised and ready to make the most of my revision time.
PUMP Phase 2: UNDERSTAND	Strengthen your Understanding and capture it in comprehensive Revision Notes.	My subject coverage is complete and I get it all! Now let's get it in a shape I'll be able to remember.
PUMP Phase 3: MEMORISE	Condense Notes into Summaries to make key information stick. Review + Recall = Remember.	I've pulled out the important bits in each subject and I can feel my brain filling with knowledge.
PUMP Phase 4: PRACTISE	Apply what you know to exam-style questions, solidify your knowledge and master your skills.	Wow this stuff's really sinking in and I'm nailing my exam technique.

Looks fairly simple, right? Well don't be fooled. It's very simple. Four clear phases to take you from now, right up until exam day.

One PUMP fits all

So the trick is to go through the four phases: Plan-Understand-Memorise-Practise, choosing your favourite tools and techniques – the ones that suit you – at each stage. I'll show you a whole load of tried-and-tested techniques for getting the most nuggets of information into your brain in the shortest possible time. You'll just need to pick the ones that suit the subject you're studying, the type of exam you're sitting and your personal preference. Be aware of your strengths and weaknesses and use the techniques that match.

This book is aimed at GCSE and A Level students, but PUMP will work at any level of study. The PUMP approach can also be used for all exam subjects, but the way you apply it will differ slightly, depending on the subject. Some subjects are focused on understanding lots of concepts (such as Biology or Economics); some require you to demonstrate skills (such as Maths or French). I will show you how to modify PUMP for each subject.

How to use this book
Read it. Mainly. Put your Coke on it. Sit on it. Throw it at your little brother. Fan yourself with it. Whatever. Above all though, use it to get the grades you're capable of. Take a look at the companion website too www.raiseyourgrade.co.uk where you can get the templates and extra resources including:

- Revision Topic Tracker
- Exam Countdown Planner
- Weekly Revision Timetable

PUMP PHASE 1: P IS FOR PLAN

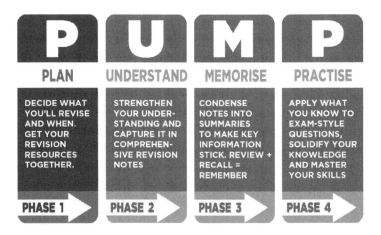

P PLAN — DECIDE WHAT YOU'LL REVISE AND WHEN. GET YOUR REVISION RESOURCES TOGETHER. **PHASE 1**

U UNDERSTAND — STRENGTHEN YOUR UNDERSTANDING AND CAPTURE IT IN COMPREHENSIVE REVISION NOTES **PHASE 2**

M MEMORISE — CONDENSE NOTES INTO SUMMARIES TO MAKE KEY INFORMATION STICK. REVIEW + RECALL = REMEMBER **PHASE 3**

P PRACTISE — APPLY WHAT YOU KNOW TO EXAM-STYLE QUESTIONS, SOLIDIFY YOUR KNOWLEDGE AND MASTER YOUR SKILLS **PHASE 4**

Failing to prepare is preparing to fail. Cliché? Yep. True? Yep.

No matter how much time you have left between now and your exams, time spent planning is always time wisely spent. Whether you've a couple of days or a couple of months, planning lets you squeeze every last drop out of your available time. Planning is for sizing up the lake of revision you're about to fall/ belly flop/dive elegantly into:

- Breadth: Planning is the only way to make sure you give enough attention to all your subjects and all the topics in the curriculum.

- Depth: Planning shows you how much detail there is behind each subject and topic and how far down you'll need to go.
- Distance: Planning shows you how long you have to keep going for, how fast you have to swim and how you can best pace yourself.

So get planning. You'll find it's the smartest few hours you ever spent.

In this Phase, you will:

✓ Step 1. Decide when to start
✓ Step 2. Get your revision resources together
✓ Step 3. Create Revision Topic Trackers
✓ Step 4: Decide how long and when you will study
✓ Step 5. Create an Exam Countdown Planner
✓ Step 6. Create a Weekly Revision Timetable
✓ Step 7. Prepare your Revision Sanctuary
   o   The Perfect Study Crib
   o   Sound or silence?
   o   Study buddies

Step 1: Decide when to Start

The only hard and fast rule here is that it's never too late and it's never too early. If you think you've left it a bit late, don't panic, just focus on making the best possible use of the remaining time. If you think you've got ages, are you sure?

We asked our 25 A-graders how far out from exams they started revising. The answers ranged from one week to 12 weeks. Proving that there is indeed no hard and fast rule. In an ideal world though – one with sunshine, world peace and free chocolate – you'd start your revision several weeks in advance of your exams.

Exactly how much time you need depends on a whole range of factors that are unique to you, such as:

- **How well organised are your Class Notes?** If your notes are all over the place with gaps the size of China, you'll need to invest more time upfront getting your notes in order.

- **How well did you understand things as you went along?** If you struggled to grasp big chunks of the course, you'll need to allow time to complete your Understanding. The earlier you start, the more time you can devote to tackling tricky topics.

- **How much do you already know?** Revising stuff you already know will give you a nice little ego boost but you really need to focus on the bits you aren't that good at. Be honest, how much do you already know?

- **How many hours of revision can you take in one day?** Will you prefer shorter bursts over a longer period, or can you manage marathon revision sessions?

```
MYTH: If you start too early, you'll make yourself
more nervous.
FACT: The more you do early on, the less pressure
you'll be under later. Getting ahead = sense of calm
(sound of Buddhist chanting). Getting behind = sense
of panic (sound of chewing fingernails).
```

```
MYTH: If you start too early, you'll just forget
everything.
FACT: Memory works by repetition, so the earlier you
start, the better. Memory works by repetition, so the
earlier you start, the better.
```

MYTH: If you start too early, you'll burn out.

FACT: If you start steady and ramp up the intensity of your revision nearer the exams you won't burn out. Also, if you do feel revision is getting on top of you, you can afford to take some time off from your books to recharge your batteries.

Step 2: Get your revision resources together

The best chefs assemble their ingredients before they start rustling up nosh. You don't see Jamie Oliver popping out to Tesco because he forgot the fresh basil do you?

So, before you do anything else, gather your supplies. I'm not talking about tinned food, bottled water and loo roll (it's revision not the siege of Leningrad), I'm talking about:

1. Stationery
2. Class Notes and Text Books
3. Revision Guides
4. Online Resources
5. Extension Texts
6. Exam Materials

1. Stationery

Remember your first day at primary school? You didn't *need* your own pens and pencils but you desperately wanted them anyway. Secondary school? New setsquare, glue stick, completely pointless bendy ruler? So you already know that every important new venture in life begins with a visit to WHSmith. Revision is no exception. You just can't beat stationery shopping to get you in the mood for revision. Here's what you'll need:

- Pens, blue/black, plus a few contrast colours (for Revision Notes)

- Pencils and pencil sharpener
- Felt-tip pens (for mind maps)
- Highlighter pens (for er… highlighting)
- Correction fluid (for er… correcting)
- Eraser (for er… you get the point)
- A4 lined hole-punched writing pads (for Revision Notes)
- Ring binders and set of dividers (for filing Revision Notes)
- Jotter pads or scrap paper (for Practising recall – and doodling)
- A5 index cards (revision cards or flashcards).

2. Class Notes and Text Books

Make sure you have a complete set of Class Notes and a copy of the core textbook for each topic. If you missed any sessions, ask your teachers or friends to help you catch up. There's no shame in a few missed classes or a lost textbook – you're a busy person – but NOW is the time to catch up and patch any gaps.

3. Revision Guides

Using revision guides like York Notes, CGP, Letts & Lonsdale, Heinemann, Collins and Longman *alongside* (not instead of) your Class Notes and textbooks can really boost your Understanding and shed new light on tricky topics.

Revision guides never waffle. They provide concise summaries of each topic and sub-topic and often explain

> "Revision guides were my primary resource for filling in gaps of understanding. They are the most concise and save a lot of time for core revision of other topics or subjects."
> *Jeffrey Poon, A-grade student*

things in a slightly different way, with fresh examples. They include exam practice material to test your knowledge and examiners' hints on how to maximise your marks.

Consider getting the accompanying workbooks that are often sold with revision guides: the more exam practice the better. You could share the cost of these with your friends since you'll only be using them once.

Revision guides vary greatly in style and quality so choose wisely. Avoid guides that claim to be all things to all people: get ones that are written for your specific exam board. Ask your teachers for their recommendations and check out forums such as www.thestudentroom.co.uk to see what other revision inmates are saying.

Oh but do resist the temptation to spend all evening in the forums bellyaching about revision. ;-)

> Warning! Don't be tempted to skip straight to revision guides instead of Class Notes and textbooks. Guides are supplements to your core material.

4. Online Resources

There are tons of online revision resources. Identify them now so you don't waste time surfing when your revision is in full swing. Some great sites for GCSE and A-level revision are:

- **BBC Multimedia GCSE Bitesize** tackles GCSE subjects in, yes you guessed it, *bitesize* chunks. You get Revision Notes for each topic, videos, games, podcasts, online tests and message boards.
- **S-cool** provides revision help for GCSE and A-level subjects and includes Revision Summaries as well as exam-style questions and answers.

- **GetRevising** is an excellent interactive website where you find, create and share study resources, including revision notes, quizzes and even crosswords.
- **MyMaths** is an excellent revision website for Maths at both GCSE and A-level. Good Revision Notes and step-by-step walkthroughs for exam-style problems. You can only access MyMaths if your school has a subscription though.
- **Sparknotes** provides free online notes for GCSE and A-level English revision. Detailed and well-organised revision guides for key novels, plays and poems. Character analysis, key themes and explanations of important quotes. Be warned though, examiners are looking for answers that have original insight, not rehashed Sparknotes.
- **Markedbyteachers.com** is the UK's largest library of work written by GCSE, A-level, university and International Baccalaureate A* students. There are notes, subject reviews, hints, tips and common mistakes from students and their teachers. Use these ideas as additional revision material if you're lacking inspiration in any of your subjects.
- **YouTube** has some great video content for GCSE and A-level revision. Keep 'em short though and NO wandering off to look at Britain's Got Talent audition montages.

Online resources

"For Biology and Economics there were actually quite a few useful videos on YouTube that provided a decent summary that grounded my knowledge."

Rita Teo, A-grade student

"I used a series of online lecture courses on academicearth. org to supplement certain aspects of my literature course."

Tom Nichols, A-grade student

Podcasts

"For GCSE history I found podcasts that were specific to the course I was studying; they were broken up into the relevant topics and went through everything we needed to know. They filled in the gaps in the course, and gave a slightly different approach to the topics which to me seemed more logical."

Hannah Bristow, A-grade student

Wikipedia

"I used Wikipedia a lot, which though perhaps not very academically sound was useful to grasp the basics of a topic."

Daisy Gibbs, A-grade student

"I found it comforting to read a Wikipedia article or another summary on the net, and realise that I knew a lot more about the text than what was there."

Matthew Hilborn, A-grade student

Warning! Watching videos can waste a lot of your time. Stick to short videos that focus on the key points.

5. Extension Texts

Examiners love to see evidence of wider reading. However, you should choose your wider reading with care otherwise you could be wasting time. You get no credit for dumping any old random knowledge; it has to be relevant. Don't go overboard with wider reading; you'll just end up confused and overwhelmed and that's not pretty. Ask your teacher for recommendations before you go wide.

6. Exam Materials

Exam boards set and mark exams. They're not evil. They actually want you to do well. They scour exam papers looking for reasons to give students good grades. It makes exam boards sad to see potential brilliance going to waste. Just to prove it they produce piles of mega-helpful resources to help you. After this book, exam materials are the absolute best things you can use to get the grades you want.

Find out from your teachers which exam board (or awarding body) is setting each of your subjects. Go to the exam board website and get downloading:

- The **Exam Specification** (syllabus) for each course you are taking.
  - o The specification provides a comprehensive list of all the topics to be studied and the skills you need to develop. Print the exam specification for each of your subjects so you can easily refer back to it throughout your revision.
  - o The Exam Spec will include the Assessment Objectives (AOs) for each subject. These specify exactly what knowledge, understanding, skills and

abilities you must demonstrate to the examiners in the exam. Your teachers will have had the AOs in mind while teaching you, and the examiners award marks based on how well you demonstrate them in the exam.

- **Past Papers** for each subject you are taking.
  - o These give you a clear Understanding of the format of each exam. It's important to see these early, during the planning phase of your revision, so that there'll be no smack-in-the-face surprises on exam day and you can tailor your revision tasks to your exams.
  - o The format of exams can change from year to year so make sure that you download only those past papers that reflect the current format of your exam. Your teacher can advise you on this. Remember:
    - o Reading past papers is a guaranteed heart-stopping, gut-wrench (Butterflies? Never was a word less appropriate). Do not freak out and do not attempt to answer any past exam questions. You're not ready yet. All you're looking for is a general idea of what you're aiming for with your revision.
    - o Knowing the format of the exam helps you tailor your revision time. For example, the way you revise for multiple-choice exams is different to essay-based exams. If you know that your exam will contain multiple-choice questions, you will focus on the key facts and

details such as terms, concepts, vocabulary and definitions. But if the exam will call for essay questions, you'll need to think about potential essay topics and how to wax lyrical on them.

o So find out:

- How long is the exam? Is it divided into sections?

- How many questions do you have to answer? Will you have a choice? Are there any compulsory questions?

- Are the questions multiple choice, short answer, essay, problem-solving or data interpretation?

- How many marks does each question or section carry? How much time would you allocate to each question?

- Is it an open book exam where you're allowed to take in notes, texts or other reference materials into the exam room? Will formulae be provided or do they need to be memorised?

- Are you expected to use specific equipment, e.g. scientific calculator, protractor, compass, etc.?

- **Mark scheme:** Understanding how points will be awarded is crucial for revision. Tips on how to make the best use of mark schemes are in *Phase 4: Practise*; you will use the mark scheme to mark your answers when you practise past exam papers.

- **Examiners' reports:** This is where examiners spill the beans on how past candidates have performed to help you avoid the same mistakes.
- **Specimen/model answers:** Looking at answers from (real or simulated) past candidates work helps to clarify the difference between an A* and a C grade. This can help you see how much work you need to do to in order to get the grade you're after.

> Warning! Remember, we're still in the Planning phase here. You should only be gathering your revision resources. It's not time to hit the books just yet.

Exam Boards, not evil

Exam boards set and mark examinations. Schools and colleges are able to freely choose between them on a subject-by-subject basis so you could have different Exam Boards for different subjects. There are six major Exam Boards that offer GCSE and A Level exams:

 Assessment and Qualifications Alliance (AQA) www.aqa.org.uk

 Council for Curriculum, Examinations and Assessment (CCEA) www.ccea.org.uk

 Edexcel (Pearson Edexcel) www.edexcel.com

 Oxford, Cambridge and Royal Society of Arts Examinations (OCR) www.ocr.org.uk

 Welsh Joint Education Committee (WJEC) www.wjec.co.uk

 Cambridge International Examinations (CIE) www.cie.org.uk

Exams from the different exam boards broadly cover the same topics but there are some differences, particularly in the format of exams.

Step 3: Create Revision Topic Trackers

How are your organisation skills? Is your desk all nicely OCD: neat row of sharpened pencils, files all labeled, colour-coded and shelved in rainbow order? Or is your workspace more of a loosely themed collage of textbooks, crumpled bits of paper and biscuit crumbs?

Wherever you are on the Librarian/Laidback spectrum, revision definitely calls for some kind of organisation. If you're not really a checklist and tick-box kind of person, it might be time to morph into one, just for the next few weeks.

Because to stay on top of your revision, track your progress and give yourself a regular sense of completion, it really helps to have a system. I recommend this one: the Revision Topic Tracker. Download and print a Revision Topic Tracker template from www.raiseyourgrade.co.uk and make one for each of your exam subjects. Here's one for 'Core Science'.

Revision Topic Tracker

Subject: **Core Science**

Revision Topics:	Complete Class Notes	Revision Notes	Revision Summary
		Revision Materials	
Human Biology	✓		
Evolution & Environment	✓		
Products from Rocks	✓		
Oils, Earth and Atmosphere	✓		
Energy & Electricity	✓		
Radiation & the Universe	✓		

The left-hand side of the Revision Topic Tracker lists the main topics for the subject. The right-hand-side shows the three sets of revision materials that you will produce for each topic, starting with your Class Notes. You will create Revision Notes and Revision Summaries in the later stages of your PUMP Revision approach – more on that later.

As you produce each set of revision materials, be sure to tick it off in your Tracker. For example, once you have a complete set of Class Notes for a topic, tick. This will give you an inner glow, a sense of progress and regular little "Well Done Me" boosts as you plough through your revision.

Another A-grade organisational technique is to create a revision ring binder for each subject. Label the spines and fronts clearly so you can grab the one you want quickly. Here's what they're for:

- Your Revision Topic Tracker – at the front, or even stuck on the front
- Class Notes on each topic – separated by dividers
- Revision Notes for each topic – separated by dividers
- An Exams section – for past exam papers, mark schemes and other exam-related materials.

Step 4: Decide how long and when you will study
How many hours a day should you revise?
It's not about how many hours you spend revising, but about how effectively you revise. Revision time doesn't earn you grades, *productive revision* does. Ignore how much revision others are doing and do what feels right for you. When I asked A-grade students how many hours they revised per day, the average was: 3 hours on a school day and 6 hours on a non-school day. Whilst

this might provide a decent benchmark, there was a considerable range across the respondents, proving that there is no right or wrong way.

> **MYTH**: You have to spend every waking hour revising to get top grades
> **FACT**: Never ever spend the whole day revising. You'll become a shriveled zombie husk of a human. People revising for 12 hours or more each day, can't possibly be working productively. Even employees don't slave that much, unless they're trying to impress the boss. And then they're only pretending.

How long should each revision session be?

The length of each revision session should depend on the length of your concentration span. Try 50-minute revision sessions, punctuated by 10-minute concentration breaks and one-hour meal breaks. If you have a short attention span, go for shorter sessions, e.g., 20-minute sessions, with a 5-minute break concentration break and one-hour meal breaks.

Non-School day example

9:00-9:50am	[50 mins] Revise
9:50-10.00am	[10 mins] Concentration Break
10.00-10:50am	[50 mins] Revise
10:50-11:00am	[10 mins] Concentration Break
11:00-11:50am	[50 mins] Revise
11:50-12:00pm	[10 mins] Concentration Break
12:00-12:50pm	[50 mins] Revise
12:50-1:50pm	[1 hour] Lunch Break
1:50-2:40pm	[50 mins] Revise
2:40-2:50pm	[10 mins] Concentration Break

2:50-3:40pm	[50 mins] Revise
3:40-3:50pm	**[10 mins] Concentration Break**
3:50-4:40pm	[50 mins] Revise

By 4:40pm you're done. The whole evening is free for relaxing.

School day example

5:00–5:50pm	[50 mins] Revise
5:50-6:00pm	**[10 mins] Concentration Break**
6:00-6:50pm	[50 mins] Revise
6:50pm-7:50pm	**{1 hour} Dinner Break**
7:50pm-8:40pm	[50 mins] Revise

Don't skip breaks thinking you're being all virtuous and super-committed. Breaks will actually help you get more done. Studies have shown that we remember more information from the beginning and end of study sessions. So instead of revising for, say, 90 minutes solid, it is better to revise for 45 minutes have a 10-minute break and revise for another 45 minutes. The more beginnings and endings you have, the better your brain will be able to remember.

What is the best time of day to revise?

The best time of day to revise is different for everyone. Your energy, mental alertness and motivation fluctuate throughout the day. When are you are the most mentally alert and focused? When do you fight fatigue and lack concentration? Don't revise late if you're not a night owl and don't get up at the crack of dawn if you're not an early bird. By revising at your peak learning times you'll learn more and enjoy it more.

"I wouldn't revise past 9pm as I found I couldn't concentrate unless it was for Maths or something where I wasn't memorizing."

Elizabeth Roe, A-grade student

"I would revise after tea there were fewer distractions; there was no good TV on until around 8pm."

Benedict Dyer, A-grade student

"Early morning revision makes you feel like you've accomplished a lot by lunchtime!"

Emily Motto, A-grade student

"I'd experience a real slump in concentration from after lunch to 4ish. Everything I did around then took me much longer than usual. Then concentration started to pick up again."

Morganne Graves, A-grade student

"I prefer working during the daylight hours as I felt more awake and engaged and I prefer working in natural light. I also think it was helpful to treat my day like a regular school or work day by not revising after dinner and giving myself time to unwind."

Maria Newsome, A-grade student

MYTH: Early risers are always more productive
FACT: Only if you're a blackbird. Some people work best in the morning, some work best in the evenings. It all depends on your Circadian rhythms you see. OK I'm losing you. Move along.

Be practical about the time of day you revise. At what time of day are there fewer distractions and interruptions?

End your final revision session at least one hour before you go to bed, otherwise you might find it difficult to sleep. German sleep scientists[1] proved that sleep is particularly crucial for consolidating newly acquired information in our long-term memory. They also demonstrated that our sleeping brains continue working on problems that may have baffled us during the day and the right answers come more easily after eight hours of sleep. So get some Zzzzzs to get some As.

Whatever you decide about the best time of day to revise, get into a routine – once you get into the habit of it, revision becomes so much easier.

Step 5: Create an Exam Countdown Planner

The Exam Countdown Planner covers the whole revision period right up until your last exam. Think of it as revision Sat-Nav (minus the annoying voice commands). Tell it where you want to go, choose your route, include the odd fuel break and Costa Coffee and off you go. Without it, you'll just end up in a field of cows somewhere.

Do the following and watch your Planner miraculously appear:

1. Download and print an Exam Countdown Planner template from www.raiseyourgrade.co.uk.
2. Fill in the dates of your exams. If you don't know these, you can find them at www.education.gov.uk/comptimetable, which collates exam dates from the exam boards.
3. Fill in your time off from school/college, e.g., Easter holidays, half-term break, study leave…

1   Wagner U, Gais S, Haider H, Verleger R & Born J (2004) "Sleep inspires insight." *Nature.* 427(6972):352-355.

4. Note down out key events that will stop you revising, e.g., careers conventions, family holidays, that big day out…

5. Look over your completed Planner. BUT OMG DO NOT FREAK OUT. You do have a proper marathon ahead of you it's true. But take it mile by mile with the PUMP step-by-step process. Breathe and proceed.

6. Stick your Exam Countdown Planner on your wall. You can colour it in if you like. #morewaystoavoidrevision ;-)

Step 6. Create a Weekly Revision Timetable

Another planner? What's this one for? A different dimension? A parallel universe? No, this one allows you to plan your revision for the week ahead.

Creating a revision timetable might feel like a waste of precious time, but it's not. Revision timetables help you break up your revision journey into manageable chunks; you make satisfyingly fantastic use of your time and you stay right on track.

1. At the beginning of each week, create a weekly revision timetable to plan the next seven days. Download and print a pile of weekly revision timetable templates from www.raiseyourgrade.co.uk.

2. Decide how many hours you will revise each day. Be ambitious but be realistic. Allow for your other commitments such as school, sports, jobs and chores. Give yourself regular time off for fun and relaxation. Add in decent meal breaks and quick concentration breaks.

3. Think about what time of day you want to revise. Work with your natural energy fluctuations.

4. Mark in the exact timings of your revision sessions (e.g. 9-10am, 10-11am etc.). Add in all your breaks.

5. Now fill in the subject you intend to revise in each session. Better still, schedule specific topics to cover in each revision session. Think about the number of revision sessions you're allocating to each subject; you should allocate more time to:

   o Your weakest subjects (revising subjects you know well makes you feel good but won't improve your grade)

   o Those that are inherently more difficult to revise (e.g. lots of terms and concepts)

   o Subjects you covered a long time ago and are less fresh in your mind.

6. Look at the *order* in which you're revising your subjects.

   o Revise for your earliest exams first. Put in more revision sessions for subjects in the days just before the exam.

   o Get your weakest topics out of the way early on when you are under less pressure and then move to the topics you feel more comfortable about. Never leave subjects that cause you anxiety till the last minute.

   o Vary your topics throughout the day to avoid getting bored. This also allows you to review topics regularly – reviewing helps commit information to memory.

   o During the early stages of your revision when you are building Understanding, you might need to continue with the same topic for multiple sessions to get momentum. Later on, when you need to memorise material, mixing up your topics becomes more important – spacing out your reviews of a topic is proven to help you remember it better.

o Tricky topics and tasks require more energy and concentration so schedule them when you are likely to be at your most productive.

o Consider how topics link to others: in many subjects, topics build on previous topics, so it makes sense to revise topics in the order they were taught.

> "In some subjects, including modern foreign languages, mathematics and science, each new concept introduced builds successively on more basic previous knowledge and understanding."
>
> Ofqual

7. Add up the number of revision sessions you have allocated per subject – does it sound balanced? Adjust your plan until it does.

8. Set yourself realistic and specific mini-goals for each session or each day. Experts say that achieving goals, no matter how small, causes a release of dopamine in your brain, leading to greater concentration and inspiration for more success. Don't argue with neuroscience – set goals!

9. Now add mini-rewards for your mini-goals. For example, after completing Revision Notes for your toughest topics, pop to the shops and get a Curly Wurly. After doing a practice exam question, upgrade to a Crunchie. Cos who needs teeth when you've got A-grades?

Remember the revision timetable is a tool for you to use, not a stick to beat yourself with. Write it in pencil. You will probably be continuously moving things around, reassessing and updating.

Breaks: The importance of planning when NOT to revise

When you're feeling the pressure, it's tempting to skip breaks and soldier on. Don't. Study breaks actually help you learn more. And you can tell that to your parents when they see you pop up in the kitchen for a sandwich – again. "Breaks are in my revision contract, Dad. Have your lawyer take a look."

Breaks give your brain a chance to absorb the material you've just covered. They also zap tension in your mind and body and give you a bit of energy zing when you sit back down. Apart from the zap and zing, it's much easier to face a day of revision when you know you've got some chunks of me-time lined up.

So here are some tips for making the most of your breaks:

- **Time yourself:** Use a timer on your phone or watch to set break alerts. That way, you don't have to keep interrupting your work to check the time.

- **Concentration breaks:** When the timer goes off: get up, stretch and get away from your desk or work area. Don't just wander round the house like a lost soul for 10 minutes; make yourself a drink or a snack, get a change of scenery, soak up some daylight, suck in some fresh air. Research shows that physical activity increases concentration and productivity by increasing blood flow to the brain, so move it!

- **Longer breaks:** Reward yourself for your revision session. Watch an episode of your favourite TV show, blast out some music, walk the dog, make contact with humans, meet a friend, make a call or send a text. Check Facebook. Check Twitter (though DO set yourself a specific time limit and stick to it – how 2 hours on FB can seem like only half an hour in RL).

- **Hit the gym then hit the books:** Recent research[2] showed that moderate exercise improves brainpower: short bursts of exercise (10-40 minutes) lead to an immediate boost in concentration, mental focus and cognitive performance, likely by improving blood flow and oxygen to the brain. So try scheduling revision within an hour after exercise.

- **Days off:** Take your days off seriously. Take a *proper* day off, completely away from your revision. Arrange to do something you enjoy. Relax and have some fun! Go nuts! You deserve it! Hell, you need it! Get out of the house, blow off some steam and come back to your revision with ruffled hair, red cheeks and renewed energy.

- **Go guilt-free:** If you feel a bit guilty taking a break, it could be because you haven't been quite as self-disciplined as you'd hoped. Forgive yourself: you're only human. Just make a fresh start next time you sit down to revise. Research shows that our brains are wired to give up on a mission if we miss a short-term goal. So, if you have a bad revision day, reflect on all the good days that you've accomplished so far and stay focused on the long view. If you keep missing your goals, it could be because you've overstretched yourself. Make sure your

2   Verberg et al. (March 2013) "Physical exercise and executive functions in preadolescent children, adolescents and young adults: a meta-analysis." *British Journal of Sports Medicine*

goals are realistic: timetables can always be revised you know.

> "I would sometimes go for early morning gym sessions and I found that my revision straight afterwards was really effective – I found it much easier to concentrate for longer periods of time and was much more focused."
>
> Emily Motto, A-grade student

> "When things got really rough, when I couldn't understand an issue at all, I would take a break, go for a run and come back. This doesn't mean when I came back I would have the answer but it at least calmed me down and made me realise that there are other ways I could perhaps find the answer (call friends etc.)"
>
> Rita Teo, A-grade student

Step 7. Plan your Revision Sanctuary

If you have a normal busy, noisy home crawling with younger siblings or a DIY-mad dad, you need to plan your revision sanctuary carefully. And get everyone to be more shushy.

1. The perfect study crib

Get comfy

You'll be sitting for long periods, so to avoid aches, pains and a really attractive hunchback situation, choose a frequent study spot that allows good posture. According to the ergonomists (comfort boffins), you need:

- A straight-backed chair high enough so that your thighs are roughly parallel to the floor and your feet are flat on the floor. If the seat cannot be lowered, use a footrest (or funky platform shoes) to provide support for your feet. And don't cross your legs for hours on end. And sit up straight.

- A chair with lower back support to help maintain the natural S-shape of your spine. No spinning bar stools for you.
- Unless you have freakish body proportions, the seat of your chair should be about 20cm lower than the desk for good posture.

A Goldilocks zone

Nothing to do with bears. I mean a room that is neither too hot nor too cold. Room temperature has a proven impact on learning performance: too tropical and you'll nod off; too Siberian and you'll find it hard to concentrate.

Natural light

Where possible, study in a room with good natural light. Daylight has been shown to improve learning, enhance concentration, increase alertness, boost energy levels and happify things generally. Sunlight is particularly good for happification. Plus you'll avoid Revision Skin Tone (somewhere between Vampire and Porridge).

Give me space

For the early stages of revision (mainly Phase 2: Understand) it will be useful to have a spacious desk area with room to spread out your work and look at several resources at once.

Get to bed. Not.
If you revise in your room, don't be tempted to revise on your bed. It's best to separate your room into distinct areas: working (desk), chillaxing (bed, beanbag, floor).

Change of venue
You might be planning to lock yourself away in your room for the whole revision period. Turns out this is not such a good idea. Research suggests that studying in different places improves memory retention. If you study the same material **once in two different places**, you'll be able to recall the information much better than if you studied the material **twice in the same place**. (You might need to read that again). Anyway the point is, our brain makes associations between what we are studying and the environment we are in while studying it. So if you revise Stalin on the sofa, recalling the sofa can help you recall Stalin. Who knew? So rotate two or three favourite revision spots: your room, the kitchen table, school common room, public library, park bench, your local Starbucks.

Banish distractions
Studies show that, once concentration has been broken, it takes 15 minutes to get it back. Now where was I...? Oh yes. Revise somewhere with minimal interruptions. Switch off your phone, TV, kid sister, hamster in his little wheel, whatever it takes.

Right, so that completes our wish list for the ideal study environment. Of course, not all of us are a stone's throw from the library and have the dosh for a daily Starbucks. Don't fret. Anything *can* work - just make the best of your situation.

Where the A-graders hit the books

"At home I prefer to revise in the kitchen, so that I don't feel too cut off from the rest of the family - they know not to disturb me when I'm working."

Daisy Gibbs, A-grade Student

"The bedroom is probably the easiest as you do not have to worry about mess so you can spread work all over the floor. The living room was a nice change of scenery when the house was empty, and being close to the kitchen, made it a nice place to snack."

Benedict Dyer, A-grade Student

"I like to a find a base and stick to it, so when I come back I know everything is where I left it and I can pick up where I left off. Sometimes though, I would have multiple ring-binders open simultaneously, so I'd work at the kitchen table."

Hannah Bristow, A-grade Student

"I changed location every couple of hours as it gave me a break when walking between the places, but also sped up my revision, as I would try to finish a certain amount before I moved on to the next location."

Emily Motto, A-grade student

"Away from my laptop and phone! I tended to leave them outside my room while revising as I found them distracting."

Maria Newsome, A-grade student

"Always in my room; I think it's important to build a sort of 'atmosphere' of hard work in one particular place, so that I could be assured that when I sat down at my desk, my brain knew that it was time to properly concentrate."

Morganne Graves, A-grade student

2. *Sound or Silence*

Music while revising: help or hindrance?

Discuss, with reference to at least 100 recent scientific studies.

For some reason, this subject fascinates the long-beardy academics, so there is a lot of research on whether music helps or hinders learning. But don't worry, I've read it all so you don't have to. Here's what I found.

Mozart Schmozart

First let's lay this one to rest. You've probably heard of the 'Mozart Effect', the idea that listening to classical music can boost your brainpower. This idea exploded in popularity after a US experiment in 1993 on the impact of listening to classical music before a test. The study found that students who listened to a dose of Mozart's *Sonata for Two Pianos in D Major* had a short-term improvement in spatial reasoning scores[3].

The study sparked a media frenzy and overblown claims were made that listening to Mozart could permanently improve your IQ. The New York Times published headlines such as 'Mozart makes you smarter' and 'Mozart makes the brain hum'. When hearing about the 'Mozart effect,' Governor Zell Miller of Georgia, in the USA, even pledged to provide every newborn baby in the state with a classical music CD. However, the study that led researchers to the 'Mozart effect' has now conclusively, utterly and embarrassingly exposed it as one of science's greatest myths[4].

---

3   Spatial reasoning plays a large part in subjects such as Math's, physics, art and design technology, engineering and ICT.

4   Jakob Pietschnig, Martin Voracek, Anton K. Formann. "Mozart effect-Shmozart effect: A meta-analysis." *Intelligence*, 2010; 38 (3): 314

Music during study

The potential benefits of music during study are that it can lift your mood, reduce stress and relieve boredom; important factors for effective study. The downside of music during study is that however much it boosts your mood, it uses some of your mental processing power. The real answer to whether you should listen to music while you study is 'it depends'. It depends on you and your individual circumstances. You need to weigh up the costs and benefits:

- Do you need music to keep you pumped for study?
- How long is your attention span?
- Are you the type of person that finds music distracting or are you able to screen out distractions?
- Does silence drive you nuts?
- Do you need to drown out background noise?

If you do choose to go with the music, all the research points to slow music with no lyrics. Save the Eminem for breaks then. Experts say music with lyrics is detrimental for studying: your brain dedicates too much processing power to them. So instrumental it is then, but not fast or loud. A Canadian study found that fast or loud instrumental music disrupts reading comprehension; soft or slow classical music does not[5].

Some types of music have been shown to actually *improve* learning. Instrumental music from the Baroque era (around 1600-1760), such as that composed by Bach, Vivaldi and Handel enhances memory retention. Unlike the fast, arousing sound of Mozart, music from the Baroque period is slow and gentle. In the 1950s and 1960s, Bulgarian neuroscientist

---

5   Thompson, W.F., Schellenberg, E.G., & Letnic, A.K. (2012). Fast and loud background music hinders reading comprehension. *Psychology of Music, 40*, 700-708

Dr. George Lozanov proved that instrumental music from the Baroque period helped students learn foreign languages in a fraction of the normal learning time. Most Baroque music has a steady tempo of 60 beats per minute. Music at this tempo is thought to put you in a 'bright and breezy' frame of mind that helps you study more effectively.

Here are some examples of Baroque music:

Bach (1685-1750)

- o   Air on the G String, Orchestral Suite No. 3
- o   Clavier Concerto BWV 1056: Largo

Vivaldi (1678-1741)

- o   Guitar Concerto: Largo
- o   The Four Seasons (Winter)

Handel (1685-1759)

- o   12 Concerti Grossi, Opus 6
- o   Music for the Royal Fireworks - Concerti No. 1 and 3

Corelli (1653-1713)

- o   Concerti Grossi, Opus 5
- o   12 Concerti Grossi, Opus 6

But if Baroque's not your bag, give 'ambient music' a try. Ambient music is designed to blend into the background. The early pioneer of ambient music, Brian Eno, created *Music for Airports* to soothe stressed-out travellers. You could also try listening to ambient sound compilations, such as waterfalls, ocean waves, tropical rainstorm, forest sounds, whale calls, crackling bonfires and so on. It'll either help you revise, make you need the loo or drive you up the wall.

The world's most relaxing music

So, what about after a hard day's revision or when the stress is really getting to you? Manchester trio, Marconi Union, worked with sound therapists to create *Weightless*, which is officially described by scientists as the "most relaxing track ever". It has been found to reduce anxiety by 65% and slow resting heart rates by 35%.

Some A-grade iTunes tips

"Whatever type of music, always very quietly, so I can hear it, but it's not always discernible. Normally classical as well to avoid the distraction of lyrics."

Thomas Pollard, A-grade Student

"Occasionally I used ambient noise to create non-silence. It actually helped me focus more on my work."

Tom Nichols, A-grade Student

"During the Planning & Understanding stages, I listened to music I knew well so wouldn't concentrate on the lyrics – I could nod along without focusing on what was being said. Also helped a bit with time management - if you stare into space for more than one song you feel you should get back to work, but if you have no music on, you don't have the 'jolt' back to reality when the song ends. During the Memorise stage I might listen to more background noise."

Russell Whitehouse, A-grade Student

"I have a large family that make a lot of noise and music blocked out background noise."

Susie Archer, A-grade Student

> "Whenever I finished a chapter or section I would choose a really up-beat, energetic song I loved and quickly get up and dance around just to relax for a bit before continuing so I could continue to focus on the work. It also kept the revision sessions quite relaxed and as "fun" as revision can be."
>
> Miriam Steinmann, A-grade Student

3. Study Buddies

Like exams themselves, revision is a fairly solitary pursuit. And if you're happy working alone, that's actually great. Don't get dragged into study groups just because everyone else seems to be doing it. The crucial thing is that, for each stage of your revision, you revise in the environment that works best for you.

Different stages of revision fit with different study environments. Early on you might prefer your own company, the sound of your own breathing, the scratch of your own pen. But as you get deeper into the murky bowels of revision, the hardest, darkest stages – when you start having actual conversations with yourself – you might find it's time to try a different vibe. Mix it up with the odd revision group at someone's house or grab a quick coffee with a study buddy.

Apart from forcing you to comb your hair and change your socks, getting together with others for revision can have some serious benefits:

- Relieves boredom and loneliness.
- Provides psychological support and motivation: helps you keep revision in perspective.
- Motivation: knowing that your study buddy is waiting for you can give you the nudge you need to drag yourself out of bed.

- Builds confidence: what's easy for one person is difficult for someone else.
- More effective learning: one of the best ways to learn a topic is to teach it to someone else. You can get help from others to fill gaps in your Understanding. Others bring a different perspective and have ideas you may not have considered.

The obvious danger with group study sessions is that they can quickly degrade into group social sessions. Some socializing is fine but make sure you get the study done first. Some tips:

- Choose your study buddies carefully. Avoid funny people, gossipy people (too distracting) or competitive people (too annoying).
- Try revising with someone you don't know that well, so there's less temptation to chitchat.
- Study with people that are of similar ability or you risk spending the whole time helping others rather than helping yourself.
- Only use study groups for subjects/revision tasks that lend themselves to discussion.

To study buddy or not to study buddy?

"I found study groups much more effective when we had a plan of what we were going to study, and what we wanted to achieve by the end of the session. It was also good when we all knew what we were going to study beforehand so came with relevant questions and problems we had individually come across that we could all try to solve together."

Emily Motto, A-grade student

"If I ever did work with someone else it would usually involve my explaining to them something that they didn't understand; this in itself does prove useful as, in vocally articulating a topic I found I could solidify it in my mind."

Hannah Bristow, A-grade Student

"There needs to be some form of structure to the session for it to be productive (past papers helped) and also it needed to be kept relatively short – less than 30/45 minutes. At GCSE less useful I thought due to the nature of the exams, but not bad for brainstorming facts and testing each other on word lists. Really just about exposure to the material."

Russell Whitehouse, A-grade Student

"I did try study groups a couple of times but it ended up with us all just chatting. The times when it did work were when we had for example essay plans which we did together, instead of just vague questions."

Julia Megone, A-grade Student

Recap of PUMP Phase 1: Plan

- It's never too early or too late to start revising.
- It's important to be organised and prepare your materials in advance.
- A revision timetable helps you use revision sessions more effectively.
- People who take breaks learn more.
- Set yourself goals and give yourself rewards.
- Create the right environment for study.

PUMP PHASE 2: U IS FOR UNDERSTAND

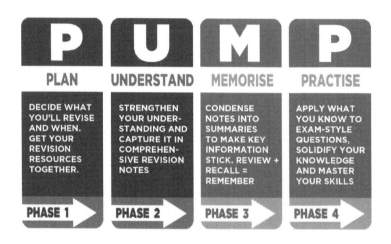

PLAN	UNDERSTAND	MEMORISE	PRACTISE
DECIDE WHAT YOU'LL REVISE AND WHEN. GET YOUR REVISION RESOURCES TOGETHER.	STRENGTHEN YOUR UNDER-STANDING AND CAPTURE IT IN COMPREHEN-SIVE REVISION NOTES	CONDENSE NOTES INTO SUMMARIES TO MAKE KEY INFORMATION STICK. REVIEW + RECALL = REMEMBER	APPLY WHAT YOU KNOW TO EXAM-STYLE QUESTIONS, SOLIDIFY YOUR KNOWLEDGE AND MASTER YOUR SKILLS
PHASE 1	PHASE 2	PHASE 3	PHASE 4

Right, you've got it all planned out. It's time to move onto the second crucial step of the PUMP Revision approach: Understand. Some students make a **BIG** mistake here: you'll see the skeletons of their shattered hopes and dreams scattered around the exam hall.

Their mistake is this: jumping to Memorising stuff, without properly Understanding stuff. They do it because they think it's a shortcut to good grades, but it's really not. They think they can simply Memorise facts and then regurgitate them in

40

the exam. But Examiners hate it when students do this. To give you some killer grades, examiners want you to demonstrate knowledge *and* Understanding.

In an ideal world, you'll have understood all your course material when you covered it in the first place. But let's face it, it's not easy to keep up with the teacher and think through complex ideas and concepts at the same time. Some days, just turning up is all you can manage.

Don't beat yourself up if you don't understand everything – you are not alone. The 'Understand' stage of your revision is your chance to build a solid Understanding of your revision topics and capture that Understanding in a set of Revision Notes.

In this Phase, you will:

 ✓ Step 1. Make sure you get The Big Ideas in each topic
  o Understand the Exam Specification
  o Understand your Class Notes and textbooks
  o Fill gaps in your Understanding
 ✓ Step 2. Create your first set of Revision Notes
  o Choose a format for your notes
  o Plan how to structure your notes
  o Reorganise the material

Step 1: Get the Big Ideas in each topic

Your first goal is to build an Understanding of the main ideas and key concepts in each topic. Here's how to start:

1. Understand your Exam Specification
2. Understand your Class Notes and textbooks
3. Fill gaps in your Understanding

Understand your Exam Specification

Before you get stuck into a topic, get stuck into the exam specification. The specification tells you, for every topic, exactly what you are expected to know, understand and be able do in the exam. This is crucial information that will help you focus your reading, prioritise your time and study each topic to the right depth.

Use the specification as a checklist to guide you through your revision. As you tackle each topic, keep referring to your checklist to make sure that you have covered every single concept, ticking them off as you go.

> **Warning!** Don't revise solely from the specification. It should be used as a checklist, not a revision guide.

Understand your Class Notes and Textbooks

Now, for each specific topic, read the relevant pages of your Class Notes and core textbook. Your textbook will provide information that your teacher may not have had time to cover in class. So, read up.

But this isn't just any old reading; this is **active reading**, where your brain is actively engaged with the content. This technique improves both Understanding and retention of the information. Quickly skim-read the material once to get the big picture and to help you navigate through it more easily when you read it in detail. Then read the material more slowly. As you read:

- Identify the key ideas, terms and concepts. Pay special attention to headings, sub-headings and summaries.

- Think about how individual ideas and concepts link together to build an overall picture of the subject.
- Link the new information to things you already know. This gives the new information an anchor that will help fix it in your brain.
- Ask yourself questions as you read (e.g., how? why?) and look for the answers in the text.
- Come up with examples and illustrations for key concepts.
- For difficult topics, look away from the text and try to summarise aloud what you've just read, as if you are explaining it to someone else. If you can't explain a topic to the cat in your own words you haven't understood it. The cat will know.

Fill gaps in your Understanding

As you read your Class Notes and textbooks, there are bound to be some topics you just can't wrap your head around. When this happens, that's the time to look at any other revision resources you've collected. Different sources explain things in a new way or provide alternative examples; this can really switch a light bulb on over your head. So look at as many high-quality explanations as possible until it 'clicks'.

Even if there are no gaps in your Understanding you can still use revision resources to build an even better Understanding. If you've grasped the basic concepts of the topic, when you have some spare time, do some extra research and read around the topic. Going that extra mile with Understanding can really get you those extra Eager Squirrel points in the exam.

Online resources are great for deepening your Understanding. So go Google. You might find some high-quality notes online from another school or college. Remember, students up and down the country are taking the same courses as you.

However, it pays to remember that anyone can publish on the web and, unfortunately, not everything on it is pure, good and true. So don't believe everything you read. Evaluate the information carefully and make sure you are confident that the information is reliable. If there's something you still don't get, ask your teacher for help. Teachers genuinely want you to do well and it's never too late to ask.

Reading around

"The gaps in my understanding could usually be filled by 'reading around', reading an extension textbook or an article. This would give the topic a little more background context."

Maria Newsome, A-grade student

" I think reading around did give me an edge in the exam - if you have a good overview of what you're studying it's easier to deal with questions that differ slightly from usual past paper questions."

Laura Bates, A-grade student

Step 2: Create your first set of Revision Notes

Before you start writing your Revision Notes for each topic, you should have read the section thoroughly several times, built your Understanding and figured out the important points to include in your notes. Everything might seem important, but in reality, there is likely to be only a handful of key ideas spread over many pages of text.

The trick is to identify the nuggets. Important ideas are easy to spot in textbooks: look out for anything in bold, with headings, underlined, given lots of space, illustrations or lots of examples. The examples themselves are not critical, so just take the nugget of the idea for your Revision Notes. So long as you understand the idea, you can usually ignore the supporting examples or come up with your own.

> "Read your Class Notes first before writing anything down – you might need to clarify points first and it's a waste of time just unconsciously rewriting notes that you might not necessarily understand or that might not even make sense."
>
> Laura Bates,
> A-grade student

So now you've unearthed the nuggets, you need to capture your Understanding of them in a set of comprehensive Revision Notes. These will form the foundations of your revision; if they are flaky, your revision will fall down. If they are strong, your revision will be solid.

The aim with your first set of Revision Notes is to combine all your resources into one new set of notes without duplications. The idea is that you will not have to refer to your Class Notes and textbooks again. Your Revision Notes will contain everything you need for the Memorise phase of your revision.

WARNING: Always create your own Revision Notes. While it might be useful to look at your friend's notes for help, don't rely on them. A) They may have missed something or not explained the topic fully. B) The process of writing Revision Notes engages the mind and you start learning sooner.

---

1. Choose a format for your Notes

There is no single 'right' format for Revision Notes. It depends on personal preference and the subjects you are taking. For biology, for example, you might want to take notes on cellular function and draw lots of diagrams. For languages, you might just list vocab or verbs. For literature, you'll have lots of quotes to learn. For History, your notes might be more like a narrative of events or a chronology. For problem-solving subjects such as Maths you might only need a few formulae. The variety is huge.

So depending on the amount and type of information you have to include for a subject, use A5 revision cards, A4 paper or A3 posters. (You don't to need go bigger than this unless you're Banksy). Take each topic one by one, find the nuggets and write your Revision Notes.

> "I bought revision cards and just went through everything that I needed to know; it really varied what subject on what they were like. For languages, for example, I used to just write vocab I needed, whereas for History it was more like a narrative of events. I really like to use loads of different colours, for dates, names etc., because it helps make the really important stuff have a separate action and therefore stick in your mind."
>
> Julia Megone, A-grade student

> "For my GCSEs I found some topics were not that in-depth, so I could write my Revision Notes onto revision cards straight away. For a lot of my A-level topics though, I would create my own mini-revision guides first. Closer to the exam date, I'd go through them highlighting and then making revision cards."
>
> Miriam Steinmann, A-grade student

Don't worry if this bit feels like it's taking ages: "OMG I'm still writing Revision Notes and I haven't even started revising yet". You have started revising. (Congratulations btw). You're capturing your Understanding in your first set of full Revision Notes. Just focus on writing great notes. Don't worry about memorising the material just yet. All in good time.

Ditch the laptop

And when I say writing. I mean writing. Old school. Pen. Pencil. One hand or the other. If there was ever a time to ditch the laptop, this is it. Why? Because handwriting is better for memory retention:

- Writing generally takes longer than typing so there's more time for your brain to digest the material (therefore you're more likely to remember it).
- With hand-written notes, there are no restrictions on how you record info: scribble notes in the margins, doodle a little picture, add arrows to show links between notes.
- Many subjects have lots of diagrams and equations that are difficult and time-consuming to reproduce on a computer.
- Handwriting during revision gives your hand muscles some much-needed training in the run up to your marathon exams.

Your notes don't have to look perfect, but they do have to be neat, clear and legible. Don't waste time making them look pretty but don't hesitate to do a second draft of the odd revision card if you can improve on its clarity. Sometimes you need a second sweep to get something right, especially with complex topics. Again, don't stress about spending time on this, you ARE revising. Right there. And you didn't even notice.

2. Plan how to structure your Notes

As you integrate material from different revision resources, give the information a clear structure so that the key points are easily accessible; it's much easier to remember well-organised information. Have a clear outline of what each topic is and what subheadings you will have for each topic.

> "Planning how to structure your notes helps you understand how different aspects of the topic link together and you can recall things better as result."
>
> Emma Brooks, A-grade student
>
> "I rigorously followed the structure of the course Specification. I did my Revision Notes following each category, so that when a question came up, I immediately knew which topic heading it came under, and recall all my knowledge in a much more organised, less frantic way."
>
> Morganne Graves, A-grade student
>
> "I would recommend dividing up topics into sub-topics wherever possible: smaller parts were much easier to remember."
>
> Maria Newsome, A-grade student

3. Reorganise the material

Make the material your own by reorganising it. Reorganising material forces you to think about it and you are more likely to remember it. Divide – each – topic – into – smaller – chunks – that – will – be – much – easier – to – r-e-m-e-m-b-e-r. It's like backwards Lego: basically you take a big and complicated thing and you deconstruct it so it turns into lots of small and simple things.

Summarising

Another important technique you will need to use in this Phase is summarising: trying to use as few words as possible in your Revision Notes. However don't get too hung up on condensing the material at this stage – focus on Understanding. You'll be condensing your Revision Notes later in your revision. Also make sure everything is in your own words because the process of rewording your Class Notes or the textbook will help you understand and absorb the information.

Make sure you know the command words that are typically used in exam questions. These are the instruction words usually at the start of exam questions that tell you what type of answer the examiner expects from you. e.g. *Explain*, *Contrast* or *List*. (See PUMP Phase 4 for more on Command Words). This will help you focus on what to include in your Revision Notes and what to leave out.

"Leave out any information that you think is obvious or unessential, because it will distract you from what you really need to concentrate on."

Daisy Gibbs, A-grade student

"Instead of just copying what you read in a revision guide or textbook into your notes, I found it better to read a paragraph, then try and rewrite what I read in a few sentences in my own words to make sure I understood it."

Susie Archer, A-grade student

Other structural tools

Depending on the subject, you might find these structuring tools useful:

- **Bullet points**: structure the main points using good old bullet points or numbered lists.
- **Themes**: where appropriate, categorise information. We humans remember things more easily if they form patterns or groups, e.g., strengths/weaknesses, advantages/disadvantages, answering the questions why/how/what/where/when, points for and against an argument etc.
- **Diagrams or charts**: summarise relationships, key concepts and ideas using diagrams or charts. Leonardo da Vinci standard not required.
- **Highlighting**: Use colour coding, underlining, *italics*, CAPS, **neon highlighting** to break up the text and make the key points easier to remember. Leave spaces between paragraphs so you don't have to read through solid blocks of writing. Make sure your notes are eye-catching, because if you remember the way the notes look you're more likely to remember what they say.

> "I used a wide range of colours, pens, font sizes, italics and underlining as well. I am actually half colour-blind, but I still found this more appealing. When I considered beginning my revision, an eye-catching set of notes was much more stimulating than a load of notes in black ink."
>
> Matthew Hilborn, A-grade student

> "I used the same colour scheme across all my Revision Notes - for consistency and to make it easier to read. All my headings were in one color, all my subheadings were in another color and indented and so on."
>
> *Rita Teo, A-grade student*

Warning! Don't look through all past exam papers. Hold some back for the Practise phase of your revision.

Examples of Revision Notes

Here's an example (from Geography) to show how the same information can be structured in different ways.

a) Using bullets

Advantages of Tourism
- Tourism brings much needed investment into an area. If it is a Less Economically Developed Country (LEDC), the foreign currency is very important to the local people.
- Tourism provides employment for many local people, ranging from working in the hotels to selling trinkets on the beach. Without the tourist industry some less developed countries would have a much greater unemployment problem.
- The money that tourism brings in can be used to improve the infrastructure of the area. New roads, airports and facilities can be built, which cater for the increasing number of tourists, but also benefit the local residents.
- Income from tourism may be used to help conserve the natural environment that is the reason why visitors come in the first place.

- The country can benefit from overseas investment, primarily in the tourist industry, but also in other related industries.
- Tourism may help to preserve local cultures and communities, as they become a tourist attraction. This is certainly the case with some Masai tribes in Kenya and Maori's in New Zealand. Both use the visitor's interest and curiosity in their culture to become a tourist attraction.

Disadvantages of Tourism
- In many resorts in LEDC's very little of the money paid for the holiday actually reaches the country. The holiday company, travel agents, airlines and hotel companies swallow most of it.
- The jobs for the locals are often badly paid, with very poor working conditions.
- The huge number of tourists coming to see it could easily damage the environment. It is very easy for a country to see the short-term economic gains of mass tourism without really taking heed of the long-term environmental damage going on.
- Increasing numbers of tourists brings problems such as littering, pollution and footpath erosion. All of these take time and money to clear up.
- Overseas investment, in things like luxury hotels, can mean that the money goes back to the country of origin. These hotels may also take trade away from local guesthouses and hotels.
- Local cultures could be devalued by tourism. They may almost become a freak show, where the visitors begin to look down on the locals as different.

Source: S-cool Revision: http://www.s-cool.co.uk

B) Grouping information into themes or categories

Advantages & Disadvantages of Tourism		
	Advantages	Disadvantages
Economic	• **Brings money** to the area • Increased **employment** of local people • Income from tourism can be used to **improve infrastructure** e.g., roads, airports etc.	• **Very little money actually reaches the country** – most of it goes to holiday companies, airlines etc. • Jobs for locals are **badly paid** with poor working conditions • Overseas investments (e.g., in luxury hotels) means **money goes back to the country of origin**
Environmental	• Tourism income can be used to help **conserve the natural environment**	• **Environmental damage** that is expensive to rectify e.g., pollution and footpath erosion
Social	• Can preserve **local communities and cultures** e.g., Masai tribes (Kenya), Maori's (New Zealand)	• **Local cultures could be devalued** – almost a freak-show

Once you have a written a full set of Revision Notes for a topic, file them in your revision binder for that subject and mark this revision task off in your Revision Topic Tracker

Revision Topic Tracker

Subject: **Core Science**

Revision Topics:	Complete Class Notes	Revision Notes	Revision Summary
		Revision Materials	
Human Biology	✓	✓	
Evolution & Environment	✓	✓	
Products from Rocks	✓		
Oils, Earth and Atmosphere	✓		
Energy & Electricity	✓		
Radiation & the Universe	✓		

Recap of PUMP Phase 2: Understand

- Develop a solid Understanding of the topic by reviewing revision resources, applying active reading techniques and writing your first set of comprehensive Revision Notes for the topic.
- Revision Notes are time-consuming and it may take several sessions to complete a topic.
- Your full set of Revision Notes for each topic may be quite long: you have combined information from all of your revision sources. The idea is that this first set of notes is fully comprehensive so you won't have to refer to your revision resources again.
- Don't get hung up on how many pages you've written. You will feel like you will never remember such a mountain of material. Don't worry, you'll be condensing your notes into smaller, more memorable chunks in the next step of your PUMP revision approach: 'Memorise'.

PUMP PHASE 3: M IS FOR MEMORISE

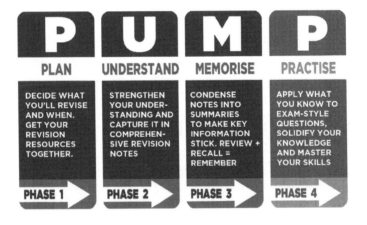

When you finish your Revision Notes for a topic, take a moment to feel the satisfaction of that. Revel in the satisfaction of your complete Understanding. Reward: half a Snickers bar.

Only half though, because Understanding is only half the battle. For most subjects, it is also crucial to Memorise. Only a combination of Understanding and Memorising will bring you exam success. Welcome to Phase 3!

Bear in mind now that phases may begin to overlap across topics and subjects. So on any given revision day you could be in Understanding mode for one subject but in Memorise mode for another. You might still be completing your Understanding of some Physics topics for example, but have moved on to Memorise for parts of Chemistry. You'll find your Revision Trackers really useful for er, tracking your revision.

Some subjects involve a lot more Memorising than others of course, but most subjects require you to learn a fair amount of information by heart. So now's the time to have faith in your brain! We all fear that we have terrible memories but, just like any other skill, Memorisation is a skill that can be learned. The trick is simply knowing *how* to use your memory effectively. This phase requires you to commit to memory all the important facts and concepts captured in your Revision Notes.

In this Phase, you will:

✓ Step 1. Condense your Revision Notes into Revision Summaries

- o Condensing
- o Mnemonics
- o Choosing the right format for Revision Summaries
    - Written format
    - Visual format
    - Q&A format
    - Audio format

✓ Step 2. Review and Recall Sessions

- o Space it out
- o Active recall

Step 1: Condense your Revision Notes into Revision Summaries

Fortunately, the act of writing your detailed Revision Notes has already planted a lot of the information in your brain. Can you feel it nestling in there? Making itself at home? Well it is.

So do I just re-read my notes?

No. Lesser students – those who settle for low grades or no grades – would proceed by simply reading or rewriting their Revision Notes again and again and hoping that it will stick. It won't. In any case, you don't need to memorise information, word for word, you need to memorise important concepts and ideas. That's where condensing comes in. So, condensing is what A-grade superstars will do next.

Condensing

With your first set of Revision Notes the goal was to take all of the relevant information from all of your revision sources and combine it into a single comprehensive set of Revision Notes without duplications. The focus was on capturing a complete Understanding of a topic. The focus now is making that Understanding brain-shaped, brain-sized and brain-friendly.

Think of it like this:

- ➲ Your Class notes, textbooks and revision guides are your full on Henry VIII Roman orgy type banquets. Lots of choice, messy, too much to eat.
- ➲ Your Revision Notes are your Mum's teas: fully balanced, meticulously prepared, broccoli and everything. Reassuring, filling, nutritious.
- ➲ Your Revision Summaries are your space-age total meal-replacement vitamin pills. Quick, easy-to-absorb, effective.

Condensing is what you do when you're trying to squeeze something big into something small, usually by removing something unnecessary. To condense Revision Notes you need to pull out the most important information and reorganise to make it easy to review and remember. Condensing is time-consuming, but stick with it. It is precisely the repetition of key ideas that makes them stick.

> "Writing Revision Notes in two stages was very useful. By making notes on EVERYTHING then making more concise notes, meant I was sure I'd covered everything I needed to know, and, but I also had some concise notes to trigger my memory of the longer ones."
>
> Emily Motto, A-grade student
>
> "I find reading Revision Notes less effective than making revision cards from them; I find I remember something better if I write it down or do something with the information rather than just reading it."
>
> Miriam Steinmann, A-grade student

> "HOW do you condense notes? I don't think I'm actually capable of doing it. Whenever I try to, I keep thinking, Oh, *well that might come up, I'll keep that.* I mean, I can make it slightly less wordy, by taking out extra words or examples, but my notes are still really long."
>
> Student post on the www.studentroom.co.uk."

Don't worry. Condensing Revision Notes is much easier than making them in the first place: you now have an Understanding of the subject and a single resource to work from. No more hunting through textbooks and Class Notes to find something. It's all in your Revision Notes.

Depending on the depth of information in a topic, create Revision Summaries on A4 sheets, revision cards or A3 posters. Reduce the material down to brief summaries of the key ideas and concepts, using as few words as possible. It might take you two or three rounds of condensing before you've really narrowed it down to the main triggers.

Your final condensed Revision Summary should be just an outline, with everything compressed into headings and key points. These key points will act as triggers to recall the essential facts in your main Revision Notes. You can then put the key ideas and concepts together to answer questions in the exam.

> "I found at this stage that my original Revision Notes were way too detailed and that I had included irrelevant information, predominantly because I had been afraid of leaving out anything useful."
>
> Matthew Hilborn, A-grade student
>
> "For my GCSEs I found that the topics were not so in-depth, so I could write my Revision Notes onto revision cards straight away. For my A-levels some topics were more in-depth so I would create my own revision guides with pictures and diagrams that someone else could use and then closer to the exam date highlight these and make revision summaries on cards writing down any facts I still could not remember."
>
> Miriam Steinmann, A-grade student

> **Warning!** Never attempt to memorise until you understand the material. 'Rote learning', where you pound information into your brain without Understanding it, is inefficient and ineffective. In exams, you will need to *apply* facts and concepts not regurgitate them.

Mnemonics

The word 'mnemonic' is derived from Greek, meaning 'to remember'. Mnemonics help you summarise and memorise material that is particularly tricky to remember. Use them with any revision format as a way of making information memorable.

> "I used mnemonics if I had to remember a list of something in a particular order, for example in history."
> Elizabeth Roe,
> A-grade student

Mnemonics appeal to your brain in two ways: first they follow a logical order (spelling a word or making a sentence); second they sometimes form bizarre or unusual words or phrases, which are therefore memorable.

Making mnemonics takes a lot of time and effort so don't waste time creating them for things that will come to you easily; create them for the stuff that is difficult to remember. Also, don't waste time creating a mnemonic if one already exists. We've included some well-known ones below; your teachers will probably have some others up their sleeve.

Mnemonics using memorable phrases

One common technique for remembering lists is to come up with a memorable phrase where the first letter of each word stands for one of the items you need you remember. A famous example of a mnemonic phrase is for remembering the colours of the rainbow: 'Richard Of York Gave Battle In Vain'. The idea is to remember a concept or list by creating fun or even rude phrases; after all only you will be using them. Some examples are below:

Physical Education: components of fitness
Cool Mums Make Fantastic Bread
- Cardio Vascular Endurance
- Muscular Endurance
- Muscular Strength
- Flexibility
- Body Composition

Music
Good Burritos Don't Fall Apart
- Bass clef line notes GBDFA
Every Good Boy Deserves Fudge
- Treble clef line notes EGBDF

Biology: Levels of taxonomic hierarchy
King Phillip Came Over For Good Soup:
Kingdom, Phylum, Class, Order, Family, Genus, Species

Mnemonic acronyms

Another mnemonic trick is the mnemonic acronym. Instead of creating a memorable phrase you create a new word. A mnemonic acronym is a word formed by taking the first letters of the series of words that you need to remember. Sometimes you get lucky and get a usable acronym from the words you need to remember, but often not. If you need to remember a list of words that doesn't need to be in a particular order, rearrange the order to help you can arrive at a more convenient acronym.

> "If there was ever a certain number of points I had to remember for a topic I would use acronyms reminding me how many points there were to make and how they all began."
>
> Megan Powell,
> A-grade student

Physical Education: Treatment method for soft-tissue injuries

RICE: Rest, Ice, Compression, Elevation

Chemistry: How electrons are lost or gained in reactions
OIL RIG: Oxidation Is Loss, Reduction Is Gain

This example shows how mnemonics acronym can also be used to help you memorise longer sections of material in your Revision Summaries. Here an acronym is used to remember the main causes of the Cold War.

History: Causes of the Cold War

BARE (Beliefs Aims Resentment Events)

Beliefs:
- Russia was a Communist country, ruled by a dictator.
- America was a capitalist democracy,
  which valued freedom of choice.

Aims:
- Stalin wanted reparations from Germany
  and a buffer of friendly states to pro-
  tect Russia from being invaded again.
- Britain and the USA wanted to help Germany
  recover and prevent large areas of Europe
  from coming under Communist control.

Resentment about history:
- USSR did not trust Britain/USA – they tried to stop
  the Russian Revolution in 1918 and Stalin thought
  that they did not help USSR enough in WWII.
- Britain & USA did not trust the USSR – Stalin had
  signed the Nazi-Soviet Pact with Germany in 1939.

Events
- Events turned mistrust into war: Yalta, Potsdam,
  Salami tactics, Fulton speech, Greece, Truman Doctrine,
  Marshall Plan, Cominform, Czechoslovakia.

{Source: CLARE, JOHN D. (2002/2013), http://www.johndclare.net}

Weird mnemonics

Sometimes you will find a mnemonic which works for you, but
to anyone else seems utterly random. No matter! Use whatever
you can. Bizarre mnemonics are often more memorable.

> "I remember learning genders for words in languages using first-letters. For example, the word for tribe in Spanish - 'tribu' - is feminine. Why? Because tribes are in Africa, which begins with 'a'. And when a word ends in 'a' in Spanish it is usually feminine."
> Matthew Hilborn, A-grade student

Mnemonics using music and rhymes

If you're a bit musically inclined, you can use this to your advantage in remembering information more easily.

> "I'd condense facts into a three- or four-word phrases which I sang or said in rhythm."
> Daisy Gibbs, A-grade student
>
> "I made up songs, particularly at GCSE level. I remembered the difference between ignite, metamorphic and sedimentary rock, for example, after having made up a song to the tune of row-row-row your boat."
> Hannah Bristow, A-grade Student

Mnemonics using Images

If the text lends itself to images, draw pictures to help you remember facts and concepts. As the saying goes, a picture is worth a thousand words. Use your imagination to liven up the information and make it easier to remember. Do this only for material that you find difficult to remember, as it can be time-consuming. #waystoavoidrevision

Anyone can create their own mnemonics - just look closely at the fact you're finding difficult to memorise, think about which type of mnemonic technique it can fit into and let your imagination run wild.

> Physics: 7 types of electro-magnetic waves in order of decreasing wavelength
> Rabbits Mate In Very Unusual eXpensive Gardens
> - Radio
> - Microwaves
> - Infra-red
> - Visible light
> - Ultra-violet
> - X-rays
> - Gamma

Choose the right format for your Revision Summaries

The trick to successful condensing is choosing the right format for your Revision Summaries. This depends on the type and volume of information you are condensing and your personal learning preference: some people prefer working with mind maps and spider diagrams, others prefer flash cards, especially for factual recall.

There are four types of Revision Summary formats:

1) Written summaries (condensed written notes)
2) Visual summaries (mind-maps, posters)
3) Q&A summaries (flashcards, quizzes)
4) Audio summaries (recordings)

1. Written Summaries

There's nothing wrong with simply writing your Revision Summaries, as long as you are condensing and paraphrasing – not copying. Read your Revision Notes carefully and identify the absolute most important ideas and concepts in each topic. Now that you have a solid grasp of the subject and how topics are inter-related, you will find that some of what seemed important earlier, when writing your Revision Notes, can now be left out.

> "Make sure every time you write something down you write it in a different way until the 'concept' sticks into your head when you condense it. This is because there is a tendency to remember information word by word in the style of the first sentence you wrote (or the textbook wrote) but when it comes to exams the question/issue won't necessarily be presented in that order of sentencing and so it is much more useful to have the key words/concepts instead."
>
> Rita Teo, A-grade student

Numbered lists

Numbered lists are helpful because they are nice and logical so they encourage the brain to always list the information in the same order, making it easier to remember.

Categories or themes

Like when you wrote your detailed Revision Notes, you should try and group information into categories or themes.

> "I made small cards, each colour coded into topics, which I stuck on my door."
>
> Morganne Hargraves, A-grade student

"For sociology A-level (which I got 100% in) it was necessary to know the name, the theory, the overarching concepts to which it was linked and the essays in which the matter would be relevant. I made dozens of pages of tables on each issue, with the four headings being literally: name, theory, concepts and essays. This really helped categorise the information in my brain, while also forcing me to condense the theory down to one paragraph. It forces you to understand and trains you to write an adequate but concise answer for each topic."

Fred Banerji-Parker, A-grade student

2. Visual Summaries

Mind maps

Mind maps provide a memorable visual overview of a topic. It has been proven that mind maps are much easier to memorise and recall than written text. Mind mapping helps to bring out the creative side of your brain and brings structure to your thinking.

Mind maps can be used to give a broad overview of many different subjects or you can create a mind map for an individual topic or sub-topic. If you want to capture a lot of information use flip-chart paper or stick several sheets of A4 together.

To create a mind map, follow these basic steps:

1) Grab a sheet of plain paper and turn it sideways (landscape).

2) Draw an image that represents the topic in the centre of the page and label the image.

3) Draw one line from the central image for each of the main points in the topic.

4) Write the main points of the topic; use trigger words or short phrases, not long sentences. Where possible, have just one word per branch.

5) Draw sub-branches stemming from each of the main branches and note down your sub-points.

6) Get creative: use images and colour-coding as memory hooks. Studies show that people who use colour when they are learning do better than those who don't. So by all means get the felt pens out but don't waste time trying to produce a work of art – the Examiner won't reward you for your beautiful mind maps and that deep sense of personal satisfaction won't get you an A-grade either. #waystoavoidrevision

7) Stick your mind maps in prominent places around your home so that you can gaze at them regularly. In the kitchen. By the loo.

If you prefer, you can create mind maps using software rather than pen and paper. Check out the mind mapping tool at www.getrevising.co.uk.

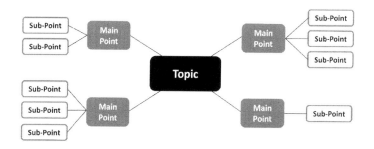

Mind maps

"I found mind mapping very useful, especially in bright colors. In exams I found myself remembering my mind map as a picture, split by different colors, and remembering what key words were drawn on it and what went where etc."

Rita Teo, A-grade Student

"I had too many notes to revise from so I used them as a basis for mind maps. I found it useful to stick them up around the house. Working in colours on mind maps helped me remember information, as I could often remember when certain notes were on each mind map relative to the colours I wrote them in."

Emily Motto, A-grade student

Posters and infographics

For subjects where you need to record information that is longer and more explanatory in nature or includes specific details, such as quotations, you might prefer to create posters or infographics. With these, you don't have to stick to the rules of mind mapping and you don't have to limit yourself to one or two words per topic/sub-topic.

Posters

"I particularly liked making posters, particularly for literature. I can remember sticking them up on the walls around my room so that I would see them and remember them constantly. But I spent too much time writing down hundreds (literally) of quotes and opinions from various critics without spending time summarising chapters or making coherent blocks of ideas that might have linked up several points into one. I do this now, but I wish I had done it then. For science at GCSE, I also used to stick up A4 sheets for every topic, but I was more efficient with this because I made sure that I would only include the key information, meaning that each point was bold and clear."

Matthew Hilborn, A-grade student

Posters

"For quotes – for English – I organised them scene-by-scene on an A3 piece of paper in different colours like a spider diagram type thing."

Laura Bates, A-grade student

"Very visual revision. Covered my walls in big colour-coded topic-split posters."

Morganne Graves, A-grade student

"At GSCE level where facts were the main focus, I used a very rigid form of mind map (Rise of Hitler), however this proved time consuming to draw and also was less useful at A-level where I needed to record information that was longer and more explanatory in nature and often included specific quotations. Instead I created A3 sheets with blocks of information, breaking the topic down into its component parts all revolving around the central title or topic."

Hannah Bristow, A-grade student

3. Q&A Summaries

Quizzes

These are useful for testing your recall of subjects with lots of facts. Create practice quizzes by transforming the key facts in your revision notes into Q and A format on a sheet of A4 paper or A5 card. Try creating some simple gap-filling exercises; write sentences with key words or facts missing and put the answers on the back. The gaps should only have one possible answer.

> "I would make mini exercises and tests, like for Chemistry, I made a game for remembering different chemical tests. I had three different coloured pieces of card: one was the name of the test, one was what the test was testing for and the third was what a positive test would look like. Then I shuffled the cards and tried to match up the correct cards together."
>
> Susie Archer, A-grade student

Flashcards

For subjects with lots of short sharp facts to Memorise, do your Revision Summaries on flash cards. They're great for carrying around and revising on the go. Flashcards are good prompts for Memorising details but don't use flashcards alone; you'll need to use other formats to capture the concepts for each topic. To make flashcards:

- **Identify the key facts** in your Revision Notes and come up with a simple Q and A for each. Write the question or prompt on one side and the answer on the other. Think Trivial Pursuit question cards.

- **Make them concise:** Each flashcard should only have one short question and one concise answer, that's why it's called '*flash*card' not '*spendagesreadingit*card'. So don't overload your cards with information. If you find you are cramming too much onto your flashcards, use written notes or a poster instead.

- **Colour-code:** Use coloured indexed cards or coloured pens to colour-code the content. This makes the material more engaging and easier to memorise. And it's pretty.

- **Add images:** Put pics on the answer side of your flashcards, to illustrate a definition for example. Studies show that we learn more from flashcards that incorporate both text and images than from flashcards with text alone.

Producing flash cards is an act of learning in itself. Test your recall by reading the prompt on the front of the card and trying to remember the answer on the back. Better still, arrange a study group quiz or get a family member to test you. In fact anyone who can read, can test you on your flashcards.

Flashcards for different subjects

- **Foreign languages:** put the vocab word on one side and the English translation on the other, with perhaps an example sentence using the word in context. Or use blue/pink cards for masculine/feminine nouns.

- **English Lit:** Use different coloured cards for different topics or for different texts in English Literature. For learning quotes, write the quote on one side and what themes/characters it refers to on the other or use the gap-fill technique with parts of the quote missing.

- **History:** Write the historical fact (key dates, places or names) on one side and concise detail on the other side.

- **Economics:** write the key terms on one side and definitions on the other.

4. Audio Summaries

If you like to learn by listening, try making an audio recording of your revision material. Audio recordings work well for self-contained chunks of information such as key facts, quotes, terminology or vocabulary for a foreign language. Try to fit what you need to know into recordings of just one minute long. Not only will you benefit from making the recording (going over the topic and speaking it aloud) but also listening to it helps fix it in your mind. You will also benefit from listening to your own voice, as people tend to be very attentive to their own voice.

The great thing about audio recordings is that you can revise with a pair of headphones wherever you are – on the way to school/ college, waiting for a bus, at the gym, on a bike ride, and so on.

Choosing the right format for YOU

So which Revision Summary format should you choose? Quizzes? Written Summaries? Audio? Visual-based ones? The answer is all and any of them!

You may have heard that we all have a particular 'Learning Style', that we are either a visual leaners (through seeing), auditory learners (through listening) or kinesthetic learners (through doing). This way of thinking has been quite widely adopted; you may have even been labeled as a particular type of learner. But the latest research shows that we don't really fit into any single box at all. In fact revising for exams involves them all. We might have a preference for the way we take in information but the evidence shows that we actually learn just as well with any learning style. So pick freely from the menu of techniques available. In fact gorge yourself. Take a bite, try them all, see which ones you like best. We learn best when we are most engaged so try and find methods that float your boat.

> "For German I recorded my essays vocally and played them back to myself."
> Morganne Graves,
> A-grade student)

Don't stick with one that bores you senseless.

Choose an appropriate format for the content you are learning

Don't revise every topic in exactly the same way. Think about which Revision Summary formats are the most appropriate for your subject matter. Studies show that we learn more from seeing the same content represented in multiple ways, e.g., Write notes, draw a mind-map, read an article, listen to podcasts, watch videos. The more senses you use, the better.

> "I think it's important to engage oneself with as many different senses as possible, and also to be active (revision can be mind-numbingly boring). Walk around, talk aloud, explain things to people."
>
> Morganne Graves, A-grade student

> "I didn't condense notes for GCSE but found it useful to condense information for A-level. I didn't get stuff down into one page for anything though really, except quotes for English, which I organised by scene on an A3 piece of paper in different colours like a spider diagram type thing. It's useful to keep everything structured, so for history I kept all my information linked to the essay structures our teacher

I kept everything sectioned- grammar, text, film, environment etc. though again I didn't use flash cards though it probably would have been useful for vocab."

Laura Bates, A-grade student

"For general grammar I made small cards, each colour coded into topics, which I stuck on my door. For vocab, I would collate it into topics. For something like History, where there was a huge amount to remember (the events, the cause and effect) I condensed everything into posters, then a skeleton timeline with all the facts, bare dates and names."

Morganne Graves, A-grade student

Once you have created your condensed Revision Summary for a topic, tick it off in your Revision Topic Tracker in your subject binder. Relish each tick. Use your best pen. Take your time. Make it last.

Revision Topic Tracker

Subject: **Core Science**

Revision Topics:	Complete Class Notes	Revision Notes	Revision Summary
Human Biology	✓	✓	
Evolution & Environment	✓	✓	
Products from Rocks	✓	✓	✓
Oils, Earth and Atmosphere	✓	✓	
Energy & Electricity	✓	✓	
Radiation & the Universe	✓	✓	✓

When you've completed a Revision Summary for each topic, you need to schedule yourself a mahoosive reward. Immediate upgrade to a Wispa Gold. Completing your Revision Summary is a big milestone in your PUMP progress. However, your work is far from done. You've made your revision materials into brain-friendly, brain-shaped and brain-ready nuggets. The next bit is where you start to upload them. Finish the Wispa first.

Step 2. Review and Recall Sessions

So, you've created a Revision Summary for every topic. You're probably thinking there's not long to go until the exams; you feel like some of it has stuck in your mind but a lot of it hasn't. You might be having a bit of a panic. But relax. Get ready for two more science-backed, student-proven techniques for getting information to stick:

- Active recall
- The spacing effect

Unless we review our learnings regularly, we forget them. You have learned some key facts through revision so far, but if you don't keep reviewing them, you will be unable to recall them in the exam.

Reviewing material not only refreshes the memory but also strengthens it, making you more likely to remember it for longer. For instance, how easy is it to remember advert jingles? Sing me the Calgon jingle now; bet you can. Washing machines live longer with Calgon! You remember it not because the tune is particularly great, but because you've heard it six million times.

Active recall

Don't just re-read your Revision Summary and think, "Yep, I know that". This gives you a poor sense of how much you really know – or worse – a false sense of confidence. According to memory experts, the most powerful technique for memory retention is something called 'active recall'. This means putting down your Revision Summary and forcing your brain to recall the information from your memory, either by writing it down or reciting it to someone. You'll be glad you condensed those notes – without condensing, there'd be way too much material.

Not only are you testing how much you really know, the act of retrieving information from memory helps reinforce it. You haven't truly learned something unless you can retrieve it from scratch. And, since that's what you have to do in the exam, that's what you'd better aim for. Studies show that students who use active recall testing greatly outperform those who just re-read the material (passive review), even when the total study time is exactly the same[6].

Don't make the mistake of believing that once you've recalled certain facts from memory they have been learned and can be dropped from further recall sessions. Recent research shows that, even after facts have been recalled once, eliminating those facts from further recall sessions greatly reduces memory retention[7]. So repetition is critical. So when you sit down for a recall session, quickly recall everything that you learned previ-

6   Roediger, Karpicke (2006) The Power of Testing Memory. Basic Research and Implications for Educational Practise. Perspectives on Psychological Science. Volume 1 No, 3.

7   Harpicke JD et al (2008) The critical importance of retrieval for learning. Science 319, 966 (2008)

ously on the topic before building on it with new information to be memorised.

Space it out

Little and often. Studies prove that you remember things more effectively if your recall sessions are spaced out over time, rather than studying the same thing like a maniac over a short period of time. This is known as the 'spacing effect'. It was a German psychologist, Hermann Ebbinghaus, who first reported the spacing effect in 1885. Decades of research by other long beards since then have proved old Dr Ebbinghaus right.

The spacing effect works because you remember much more if you review something just as your memory of it is about to fade. If you have to stretch slightly to retrieve a memory, the stronger that memory becomes. If something is still fresh in your mind you won't gain much from reviewing it.

So that's why, at this stage of revision, it's better to have short recall sessions and mix up several topics in one day, rather than devote one long session in which you go over a topic again and again, which will drive you to the brink of madness anyway.

The spacing effect requires good time management but it doesn't require additional study time, which is great seeing as you probably don't have a lot of that going spare at the mo. In fact, the spacing effect will save you time and fix the information more firmly in your brain.

The number of review sessions and the length of gap between each review depends on how many exam subjects you have and how long you have left before your exams. But aim to test yourself on everything at least twice in the run up to your exam. Give each subject a final focus the day before the big day.

"I would make sure to schedule recall sessions about two days after my main body of revision on a topic. This would force me to remember the information. I would also recommend getting someone else to help test you, particularly with vocabulary, dates or short facts."

Maria Newsome, A-grade student

"They shouldn't just be sessions. You should review, then when you're having dinner or on the bus to school, see how much you can recall, and then subsequently return and review further any gaps in your memory that voluntary recall has identified."

Thomas Pollard, A-grade student

An active recall session using Revision Summaries

Here's *how* you can incorporate the above principles into your review sessions for maximum memory retention in minimal time:

1) Choose a section of a Revision Summary you want to memorise. Read it aloud. Reading material aloud involves both the speaking and listening parts of your brain and so increases your ability to recall the information.

2) Cover the Revision Summary. Now try to reproduce the main points from memory, in your own words – write them down on scrap paper or say them out loud. If you forget something, try and visualise the page.

3) Compare your recall with your Revision Summary. Underline in pencil anything you got wrong or had trouble recalling.

4) Look at the Revision Summary again and review only the underlined information you couldn't recall.

5) Cover the Revision Summary again and try to recall ALL the main points.

6) Again compare your recall with your Revision Summary. Underline in pencil anything you got wrong or had trouble recalling.

7) Keep repeating this exercise until you have successfully recalled everything.

8) Now you are confident that you have nailed the basic facts, go back to your first set of Revision Notes on this topic. Check that the main points you have successfully memorised from your Revision Summary jog your memory and bring back the detail in your main Revision Notes. If it doesn't come flooding back, perhaps your revision summary is *too* brief. Re-read your revision notes and add additional memory triggers to your revision summary.

Remember to wait a while before reviewing this topic again (remember the spacing effect?) When you next pick up this Revision Summary for review, quickly recall everything that you learned previously before tackling a new section.

> **Recall tip**
> "Occasionally I would try and visualise page layouts of my revision, remember where a piece of information was written on a page and attempt to pick out bits of related info nearby."
>
> Tom Nichols, A-grade student

An active recall session using Flashcards

You can employ the same techniques using flashcards. Instead of studying your flashcards sequentially over and over again, try the following:

1) Select a stack of flashcards to test yourself on.

2) Test yourself on the first flashcard (i.e. try and recall the answer before flipping the card over and having a look).

3) If you get it right, put the card on the 'Right' pile. If you get it wrong, put it on the 'Wrong' pile.

4) Once you have gone through all the flashcards in the stack, pick up the Wrong pile and repeat the process.

5) Keep testing yourself on the Wrong pile until you have recalled all the answers correctly and there are no cards left on the Wrong pile. When you next review the same stack of cards, perhaps in a couple of days, start the whole process again.

Why am I doing this again?

Testing yourself means you are fixing the information in your brain. If you make a mistake you are forced to review that information more often – the easy stuff sinks in and the hard stuff keeps showing up until it is memorised. The result is that you prioritise your studying, focusing on the information that is troubling you and reducing your overall amount of study time.

Testing yourself using active recall and scheduling recall sessions to benefit from the spacing effect both require effort. It might seem easier to just re-read material again and again in big old cram sessions, but you won't learn stuff as fast or retain it as well. Trust the scientific evidence and wait for you efforts to pay off. Meanwhile pile up some mini-rewards for successful recall sessions.

"I stuck posters up all over my house, so was always surrounded by information - such as when I was making a cup of tea or brushing my teeth I could look over a poster, and then when I wasn't in front of a poster I would try to remember what the poster looked like and what was written on it. For example, if I was on the bus home from school, I might think about what the poster in the bathroom was like, and then would look over it when I got home to see if there was anything on it I had forgotten."

Emily Motto, A-grade student

"Sticking revision cards around the house is a very good one, since you read them several times throughout the day and then in the exam can take a virtual walk through your house and will associate places in your home with the information. Reading the same thing over and over for 5 minutes is a lot less effective than reading it several times throughout the day spaced out."

Miriam Steinmann, A-grade student

Recap of PUMP Phase 3: Memorise

- We remember things that are both easy to remember and repeated. So condense your Revision Notes into Revision Summaries.
- Choose a format that is appropriate to the material, that suits you and that is easy to remember (written notes, mind maps, flash cards, etc.)
- Make sufficient time for multiple review and recall sessions. Repetition is key to retention.
- Maximise memory retention by testing yourself and spacing your recall sessions out.
- Every session, repeat what you learned last time on this topic and focus on the material you have most trouble recalling.

PUMP PHASE 4 P IS FOR PRACTISE

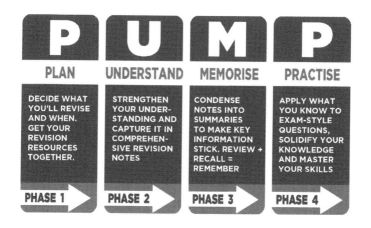

The final phase of the PUMP revision approach is Practise. This is where it all comes together. Here's where you apply what you know to exam-style questions. And by applying what you know, you realize what you still don't know.

The Practise phase puts the finishing touches to your Understanding and Memorisation. So in reality, the phases of PUMP now overlap and repeat a little:

- Doing exam questions (Practise) will highlight gaps in your knowledge (Understand) and you may need to go back to plug those gaps

- You will be Memorising right up until exam day, throughout the entire Practise phase in fact.

Importantly, the Practise phase also gives you chance to nail your exam technique. This is a crucial element for you in the run up to exam time. Even the smartest, hardest-working students will fail to get the grades they deserve if they fail to master the basics of exam technique.

To maximise your marks, you need to learn how to demonstrate your knowledge, understanding and skills under exam conditions: nerve-wracking, gut-wrenching exam conditions.

Warning! Don't move onto Practise before you have a really good Understanding of all the material. You won't be able to understand where you're going wrong unless you understand the topic first.

In this Phase, we will cover:
✓ Step 1. Get to grips with your Assessment Objectives
✓ Step 2. Get familiar with Command Words
✓ Step 3. Get the best out of past papers
  o Simulate exam conditions
  o Mark the paper harshly and address the gaps
  o Understand the mark scheme
  o Look out for buzzwords and key phrases
  o Read Examiners' reports and exemplar answers
✓ Step 4. Master your exam technique
  o Choose your questions carefully
  o Plan your time
  o Plan your answers
  o Structure your answers
  o Answer the question

Step 1. Get to grips with your Assessment Objectives

When examiners mark your exam paper, it doesn't matter if they're having a bad day or a good day. They're assessing your answers against clear and stringent Assessment Objectives (AOs). The AOs are defined by the exam regulators and specify the knowledge and Understanding of the course content you must show, as well as which skills and abilities to demonstrate. So it's vitally important to get to grips with your AOs:

- Understand what each AO means
- Know the proportion of marks allocated to each AO
- Understand how to demonstrate each AO in the exam

Here are three common AOs at GCSE and A-level, along with the OCR Examiners' definitions

AO1: Recall, select and communicate knowledge and understanding

This AO tests the information and learning you have acquired and how well you can comprehend meanings and interpret information in written or graphic form. It requires only direct recall and communication of knowledge gained by studying the specification.

AO2: Apply skills, knowledge and understanding

This AO requires you to be able to recognise when and where the knowledge you have might be useful in real life. Application is the skill of being able to apply your knowledge to different contexts and circumstances in order to understand why problems and issues arise.

AO3: Analyse and evaluate

Analysis AOs may require you to interpret data in a table, chart or diagram, identify trends or identify the elements that make up the problem, issue or case that you are considering. Evaluation AOs call for judgment and opinion; commenting on how important, significant or valuable something is. You need to demonstrate that you have the confidence to make judgments based on your knowledge.

Source: A Parent's Guide to Understanding Exam Techniques (www.ocr.org.uk)

For some exam questions, Examiners will also be assessing the quality of your written communication skills. According to exam board regulator Ofqual, candidates must do the following:

- Ensure that text is legible and that spelling, punctuation and grammar are accurate so that meaning is clear.
- Select and use a form and style of writing appropriate to purpose and to complex subject matter.
- Organise information clearly and coherently, using specialist vocabulary where appropriate.

In other words, shabby work will cost you.

Step 2. Get familiar with Command Words

Sit! Fetch! Roll over! Dogs can master a whole range of command words as long as there's something in it for them. Same for you. Your understanding of and ability to respond appropriately to Command words in exam questions will pave your way to some crunchy A-grades.

Command words are the instruction words in exam questions that tell you what type of answer the examiner expects from you. Different command words are used to elicit different kinds of responses, not just to spice things up! You need to be clear about what command words are asking you to do. For example, a command word like *Describe* requires a different type of response than a word like *Explain*.

Below is a list of some of the command words used in exam questions, with guidance on the meanings of the words, provided by Ofqual.

What they say	What they want you to do
Analyse	Separate into components and identify characteristics
Apply	Put into effect in a recognised way
Argue	Present a reasoned case
Assess	Make an informed judgement
Calculate	Work out the value of something
Comment	Present an informed opinion
Compare	Identify similarities
Complete	Finish a task by adding to given information
Consider	Review and respond to given information
Contrast	Identify differences
Criticise	Assess worth against explicit expectations
Debate	Present different perspectives on an issue
Deduce	Draw conclusions from the information given
Define	Specify meaning
Describe	Set out characteristics
Develop	Take forward or build upon given information
Discuss	Present key points
Estimate	Assign an approximate value
Evaluate	Judge from available evidence
Examine	Investigate closely
Explain	Set out purposes or reasons
Explore	Investigate without preconceptions about the outcome

Give	Produce an answer from recall
Identify	Name or otherwise characterise
Illustrate	Present clarifying examples
Interpret	Translate information into recognisable form
Justify	Support a case with evidence
Outline	Set out main characteristics
Prove	Demonstrate validity on the basis of evidence
Relate	Demonstrate connections between items
Review	Survey Information
State	Express in clear terms
Suggest	Present a possible case
Summarise	Present principal points without detail

Specific subjects have their own traditions and expectations when it comes to command words. Read the materials on exam board websites to understand what command words might be used and exactly what they mean in the context of your specific subject. Usually there is only one command word for each question, sometimes two. The number of marks available for the question will give you a further hint about the kind of answer required.

If there's a Command word you don't understand, don't just wag your tail and look cute. It's crucial to get to grips with command words so ask your teacher for help.

Examples of how command words are used in exam questions

Here are some worked examples of command words used in GCSE Science questions provided by AQA Exam Board. Below the explanation of each command word is an example exam question, with an answer which would gain full marks.

Describe

Students may be asked to recall some facts, events or process in an accurate way. For example they may be asked to describe an experiment they have done, or they may need to give an account of what something looked like, or what happened, eg a trend in some data.

Example: Biology

9   A person accidentally touches a hot pan.

Her hand automatically moves away from the pan.

The diagram shows the structures involved in this action.

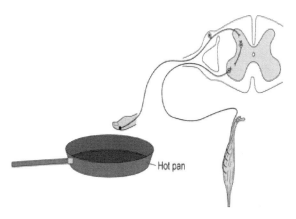

Hot pan

Describe fully how the structures shown in the diagram bring about this reflex action.

First of all the heat (the stimulus) will be detected by the temperature receptors in the skin. The receptors will then send an electrical impulse along the sensory neurone to the synapse in the spinal cord. A chemical messenger is released, which crosses the synapse space and triggers an impulse in the relay neurone. The same thing happens at the next synapse so that an impulse is sent down the motor neurone to the muscle, which is the effector. When the impulse reaches the muscle it causes the muscle to contract and pulls the hand away from the heat. This is a reflex action, and it does not have to be processed via the brain.

(6 marks)

DR DENISE GOSSAGE

Evaluate

Students should use the information supplied as well as their knowledge and understanding to consider evidence for and against. An evaluation goes further than 'compare'. For example, they may be given a passage to read and told to 'Evaluate the benefits of using system x and system y'. This means they will need to write down some of the points for and against both systems to develop an argument. A mark may also be available for a clear and justified conclusion. For example, if a question is worth 5 marks, and does not specifically ask for a conclusion, then a student can gain all 5 marks for 5 valid points made for and against. If the student only makes 4 points but gives a justified conclusion then the 5th mark can be gained.

However, if a question specifically asks for a justified conclusion then full marks can only be gained if a justified conclusion is given.

When giving comparisons students should be encouraged to compare both sides using linking words. For example in the physics question 'Wind power is a renewable resource whereas fossil fuels are non-renewable.' Useful words for students to use could be 'however', 'whereas' 'but' and 'on the other hand'.

Example: Physics

13   Wind turbines can be used instead of power stations to generate electricity.

Evaluate the use of wind turbines for generating electricity.

Wind power is a renewable source of energy which will never be used up whereas fossil fuels are non-renewable. When we eventually run out of fossil fuels we will need something to replace them. There are no waste gases from wind turbines so they do not pollute the atmosphere like fossil fuels. However they do make a noise which some people living near to them object to. Also unless you live in a windy place they will not work all the time as they don't generate electricity when the wind is not blowing.

I think wind turbines are a good idea as global warming from burning coal is an increasing problem and needs to be stopped.

(5 marks)

Explain

Students should make something clear, or state the reasons for something happening. The answer should not be a simple list of reasons.

This means that points in the answer must be linked coherently and logically. Suitable linking words could be 'so', 'therefore', 'because', 'due to', 'since', 'this means' or 'meaning that'.

All of the stages/steps in an explanation must be included to gain full marks.

Example: Chemistry

15   A mixture of the olive oil, water and egg yolk was shaken and left to stand. The olive oil and water do not separate.

The diagram shows a simple model of how a stable mixture of olive oil and water is produced by the addition of egg yolk.

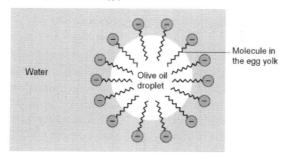

Use this simple model to explain how the molecules in the egg yolk are able to produce a stable mixture of olive oil and water.

The molecules in the egg yolk have a 'head' part that dissolves in water, but a long 'tail' part that dissolves in oil. A large number of these molecules surround the oil droplet and so it can stay suspended in the water as an emulsion which is stable. Therefore, the egg yolk molecules act as an emulsifier.

(3 marks)

Step 3. Get the best out of past papers

Do as many past papers as you can get your hands on. It is the absolute best use of your time in the Practise phase of revision. In fact don't just stick to past papers: go back to homework questions and questions you covered in class, find practise questions on the internet, in your revision guides, anywhere. You could even try making up your own questions from your notes.

> **Where to find practise resources**
> "For A2 history, I wrote and answered two of my own questions based on previous past questions. For GCSE Maths, I used the textbook and BBC Bitesize exercises. Revision guide exercises were particularly useful for A-level chemistry."
>
> Emma Brooks, A-grade student
>
> "Revision websites such as BBC bitesize were quite useful a few days before the exam since it was a way of quizzing your-self and finding any possible gaps in your knowledge. Most textbooks have end of chapter questions with the answers in the back and I redid all of these since I could then check the answers at the end. Usually the textbooks are designed for the course you study and so the end of topic questions would be quite similar to the style of the exam paper and would cover any prominent points you would be expected to know as well as a few of the more obscure facts."
>
> Miriam Steinmann, A-grade student

Simulate exam conditions

When doing past papers, it is best to simulate exam conditions as closely as possible. No need for the big draughty hall with squeaky floorboards and someone with a persistent cough at the back. Just do this:

- **No cheating**: No peeking at your Revision Notes or other aids. Always try and answer the questions before looking at the answers/examiners marks. Here's the truth: when it comes to exams, you are on your own. Literally. Desk. Pen. Paper. Big ticking clock. Little old you. It's sometimes tempting to read the question, tell yourself that you could answer it and then go look. Don't do it! The whole point is to practise recalling what you know, applying it to the question, planning how to answer it and answering it within the time available.

- **Silence please**: Work in complete silence with only the scrape of your own pen on the page. Go to the library or lock yourself in your room with a sign taped on the door – 'Silence please. Exam in Progress.'

- **Time it right**: Work out how long you will have to answer each question in the exam, based on the way marks are split. When you first attempt past papers, break the paper into several parts to create short practice sessions. This gets you used to working under time pressure and prepares you for how quickly you need to work in the exam. Closer to the exam, try whole papers under timed conditions to give you endurance practice.

What A-grade students say about past papers

"I used past papers to find gaps in my knowledge, to get a sense of what may come up in the exam and to flag up any repeated mistakes that I make so that I can avoid them – for Maths in particular."

Megan Powell, A-grade student

I used past papers to satisfy myself that I'd done enough work - it's a confidence-booster to be able to read a paper and think 'Yes, I could do this'."

Daisy Gibbs, A-grade student

> "I would attempt the paper as a mock, then I would go back through the paper with my notes to try and answer questions I could not do or improve answers that were not comprehensive enough."
>
> Susie Archer, A-grade student

> "I didn't use past papers for my GCSEs apart from Maths. For A-levels though, I did past papers under exam conditions and then revised the parts I didn't get right before doing the next paper."
>
> Miriam Steinmann, A-grade student

Mark yourself harshly and fill the gaps

Assess your answers using the examiners' mark scheme so that you understand exactly what they are looking for. The mark scheme shows you exactly why marks are awarded or withheld.

Check what else you could have written to bag every single mark. Highlight any questions you still do not understand and ask your teacher to take a look or even mark your paper.

When you get stuff wrong don't get mad, get even! For questions you got wrong or for poor scoring answers, find out why. Do you need to build your Understanding or did you simply not spot what was being asked of you? Mistakes are a crucial aspect of the learning process; it's great that you are making them now rather than later. You still have time to rectify them with hard work. Yes more, just a little bit more.

What the examiners say about past papers

"Past papers are possibly the most useful resource when revising. They enable you to gauge your subject knowledge and uncover your strengths and weaknesses, enabling you to understand which areas you need to devote more or less time to."

WJEC Examiner

"Past papers are handy for seeing the level of the questions you'll face in an exam."

Edexcel examiner

"It's like being an athlete. You're training for two years but then you've got to run the race. It's crucial that you get used to sitting down, and doing it in the appropriate time, under exam conditions as closely as possible."

George Turnbull, former examiner

Understand the mark scheme

Don't peek at the mark scheme until you have attempted the past paper. When you're marking yourself, you should devour the mark scheme. It gives you a rough guide in writing the appropriate number of points in the right depth. There are three types:

1. **Objective** mark schemes: when there is only one correct answer, e.g., a single number/word or a multiple-choice item. Right or wrong.

2. **Points-based** mark schemes: for questions requiring one or two paragraphs or a diagram. The examiner will count the number of creditworthy points you have made. So take note of how many distinct points you are expected to make in your answer to get full marks.

You might get, for example, one mark for identifying a relevant point and one for explaining it.

3. **Levels-based** mark schemes: for questions requiring longer answers, such as essays. Examiners use pre-defined descriptions to decide which one best describes the level of skill or Understanding you have displayed in your answer. They are on the lookout for certain triggers in your answers that will allow them to mark you up to the next level.

Look particularly at:

- Will you get marks for making particular points in your answer and what are the other gold coins and triggers that will earn you specific grade levels?

- Will the quality of your written communication be assessed i.e., legibility, spelling, punctuation and grammar, organising information clearly, using specialist terms where appropriate?

- Will marks be awarded for a correct method/calculation even if the answer is incorrect and will crossed-out work be marked?

```
Warning! Don't assume that the mark scheme for your
exam will be exactly the same as last year. The guid-
ing principles of assessment will remain the same but
the allocation of marks for each question may change
depending on the content of the exam paper.
```

Key phrases make prizes

The mark scheme often specifies the phrases and key words that will get you particular credit. This is only useful if you truly understand the material; do not simply commit the phrases to memory and try and regurgitate them without understanding them. Examiners can spot this a mile off. You need to be prepared for different angles and unfamiliar questions; examiners want fresh ideas, original thought and students who can think for themselves.

Read the Examiners' Report and Exemplar Materials

Once you've completed a whole exam paper, read the exemplar materials provided by the exam board. By comparing your response to that of other students you can see what you are doing well and what you need to work on. These can be a bit intimidating, but remember they *are* exemplary materials. Get anywhere close and you're onto a winner. Calmly assess your answers and learn from your mistakes.

The examiners' report is a valuable resource that highlights common mistakes made by students. It's worth a careful read to ensure that you avoid the same mistakes.

What the examiners say about the mark scheme
"Mark schemes are not intended to be totally prescriptive. No mark scheme can cover all the responses which candidates may produce."

CEA Examiner

"The marking scheme does not give examples of all possible, rewardable answers. There is almost always a range for every answer. Examiners must recognise and reward relevant material, even if it is not included in the marking scheme."

OCR Examiner

Step 4. Master your exam technique

The night before your exam, aim to finish early, chill out and get a good night's sleep.

On the morning of the exam, you could read through your Revision Summaries but only if it doesn't make you more nervous.

Never try and learn new content on the morning of the exam. Just focus on keeping calm and think positive – you can do this!

- Remember that nerves are normal – everyone feels nervous about exams.
- Remember that exams are not designed to trip you up, but to allow you to show your knowledge. The Examiners are on your side; they are looking for ways to give you the marks. Make it easy for them.
- Be positive and have confidence in your ability. Keep calm and carry on.

"Do not cram new information in the night before an exam. Relax, if you can, by lightly reading over your notes for the next day. Do not worry if you can't, most of us can't either, so you are no different - but stick to the no-cramming rule."

George Turnbull, former examiner

"Do not attempt to learn new topics on the day of your exam; instead revisit and refresh topics you have already covered. Familiarise yourself with key points, key dates, formulae or essay plans etc."

WJEC Examiner

What the examiners say about exam day

"Avoid discussing the exam with class mates at the examination venue. Talking about the exam immediately beforehand can cause unnecessary stress. Choose other topics of conversation or find somewhere quiet to gather your thoughts alone. If you panic, you cannot think straight."

WJEC Examiner

"When you arrive, avoid friends/classmates who are highly stressed; don't let their stress affect you. If you feel anxious during the exam, stop, shut your eyes and breathe deeply. Open your eyes, breathe in again and get back to your paper. If you are allowed water in your exam room, have small sips."

AQA Examiner

"Ignore the people around you that are rushing on like they are going to be finished before everyone else. It's your examination so sit it in your own way."

George Turnbull, former examiner

You may now turn over the page

These words have the potential to strike fear into the heart of the most laid-back student.

But take a chill pill: close your eyes, let your shoulders drop, take a big breath in through your nose, hold for a few seconds and slowly exhale through your mouth. This is one of the best ways to calm your mind.

The absolute best way to work through your nerves is to just get down to business. So look at your paper and begin:

1. Read through the whole paper
2. Choose your questions
3. Plan your time
4. Plan your answers
5. Structure your arguments
6. Answer the questions set

1. Read through the whole paper

Start by reading the whole exam paper from cover to cover. Do not hold your breath during this exercise, you will fall off your chair and cause a disruption.

2. Choose your questions carefully

If you have a choice of questions, take time to consider the questions carefully and select the questions where you think you can gain the highest number of marks. Mark the questions you will answer and ignore the others.

> "Look at ALL the questions. Consider what slant or aspects of the topic the examiner wants you to discuss. DO NOT choose a question because you recognise one word in it, then write a general essay you've written previously on that topic. It is very unlikely to meet the demands of the question."
>
> WJEC Examiner

Pick the right essays

Essay or longer response questions are worth a lot of marks so you really need to nail them. Before deciding which question to answer, ask yourself the following:

- Do you have enough knowledge and ideas on this topic?

- Do you have the topic-specific vocabulary to answer this question?
- Can you think of lots of examples to support your points?

> "'Yes! My favourite topic has come up!' It's always pleasing to see a topic you enjoy and find easier than other topics. Answering these questions early in the exam can help to settle some tension and nerves and help you to gain confidence for topics you are less confident with."
>
> WJEC Examiner

Start with the easy questions

Answer the easy questions first and save any difficult questions for the end – this will build your confidence and help you relax into the exam.

Read the questions twice

Examiners always say one of the most common mistakes students make is not reading the question properly. It's easy to misread things when you are nervous.

To do well in an exam, it is crucial to fully understand what exam questions mean and how they should be answered. So read it twice, underline key words, which suggest how the question should be answered:

- **Topic:** What topic is the question about?
- **Key aspect:** What slant on the topic should you take?
- **Command word(s):** What are you being instructed to do? If you are asked to 'Describe', don't waste time with explanation. Similarly, if you are asked to 'Explain' don't 'Describe'.

"Look out for the key words in a question and underline them – what exactly is the question asking you to do? Watch out too for any help being offered to you in the question itself. We want you to do as well as you can, so the questions are worded carefully to help you to focus your attention in the right area."

Cambridge Examiner

"One criticism of candidates was not reading the question properly and not understanding command words such as 'describe' or 'explain'. There was, on occasions, a lack of detail in the answers with candidates, for example, giving a list instead of an explanation."

Extract from WJEC Examiners' Report

3. Plan Your Time

There are no two ways about it: you have to work quickly in exams. You get no marks for unattempted questions, so it is crucial to plan your time before you begin writing.

1. Allocate time for each question according to how many marks each question is worth.

2. Allow yourself time to plan each question, particularly those requiring essay answers.

3. Allow time for reviewing your whole paper at the end. This is particularly important for questions with multiple calculation elements, such as Maths or Physics. But you should also review essay answers; even if you cannot squeeze paragraphs in you can tack extra information on the end, in note form.

4. Set yourself progress points so you can monitor how you're doing during the exam e.g., "At the 45-minute mark I should be on Question 2".

Timing yourself

"You will probably have much more to say than you have time to say it. I remember exiting my English exam thinking that I could have written double the amount that I was allocated time for each essay. I knew so many different quotes and contextual points. So practising timed essays from exams in exam conditions is definitely useful, if only to see how much you can physically write in the time."

Matthew Hilborn, A-grade student

Be disciplined and stick to your plan

Unfinished papers are a common reason for poor grades according to Examiners. They say that final questions are often rushed or missed out completely. Don't let time mismanagement scupper your chances of getting the grade you deserve.

Keep an eye on the clock and stick to your plan. Some flexibility is OK, but if you spend too long on one question it will reduce the amount of time you have to answer the others. So if you find yourself running out of time on something, be ruthless and move on. You can come back to it later if there's time. Leave space in between your answers so you can add to your answer neatly.

4. Plan your Answers

For longer response or essay questions, don't jump the gun. Think first about the question and plan your answer, jotting down the main points and the supporting evidence and examples. When you're time-pressured it's tempting to skip the planning stage and launch straight into your essay but an essay plan ALWAYS produces a better essay:

- Planned answers are better structured. It's easy to get lost in essays, especially under pressure. Roughly outline the general content for each paragraph and any examples or quotes you intend to use to support your answer.

- Laying out how your argument will unfold before you start your essay means you can focus on writing rather than trying to think of your next point. Planning helps you remember all the important points.

- If you run out of time the Examiner can award you marks for your plan, so make sure you write your plan on the exam answer sheet, not on scrap paper. Label it 'Answer plan' so it's clear.

- It doesn't matter whether you jot down a few bullets or structure them in a mind map. Plans can come in all shapes and sizes.

5. Answer the Question set

Don't just write down everything you know on a subject. This is called 'offloading' and examiners can spot it a mile off. No matter how splendiferous your knowledge and Understanding of a topic, if you don't answer the specific question, you get no marks. Make sure you don't answer the question you wish you'd been asked rather than the question in front of you. Keep referring back to the question, and keep your answer focused.

> "Answers must be relevant to the question. Beware of prepared answers that do not show the candidate's thought and which have not been adapted to the thrust of the question."
> OCR Mark Scheme for GCSE English Literature Exam

> "In science and mathematics based subjects, clearly show all workings out. Marks are often awarded for correct methodology even if the final answer is slightly incorrect. Write down any relevant formulae as well, as this demonstrates the subject knowledge from where you have derived your answer."
>
> WJEC examiner

Don't over-answer the question

Take account of the number of marks allocated to each part of each question and write answers of appropriate length. Don't write more than required just to prove how much you know. An examiner can only award full marks, even if you have written eight pages of fascinating and relevant material. There are no bonus prizes for quantity, so use your time wisely.

> "Many candidates spend too much time earning and re-earning small numbers of marks, losing time for the heavier-tariff tasks. Remember, answering three questions fairly well is better than answering one very well and leaving two badly done."
>
> Edexcel examiner

Show good use of English

For written responses get the examiners on side by showing good use of English. That means proper sentences, not a list of bullets.

> "Unless you are really pushed for time, don't answer a question by just giving a list or using bullet points. The examiner will be expecting you to show good use of English and if you use bullet points you will not get the highest level marks no matter how good your knowledge or understanding."
>
> WJEC Examiner

Jot down ideas as they come to you

If you're answering a question and information relevant to another question pops into your head (a fact or mnemonic for example) just jot it down. Otherwise trying to remember it could distract you, or you might forget it by the time you get to the relevant question. Let things just ping into your brain and ping out of your pen until you need them later.

Review Your Answers

Once you have completed a question, read through your answer. It is easy to make silly mistakes when you're under pressure.

- Check for obvious mistakes
- Have you answered the question?
- Grammatical errors?
- Spelling mistakes?

Do not be afraid to make corrections, using carats (^) or asterisks (*) to add extra material above the line or at the end. Do not be afraid to put a line through words and make a clear substitution.

> "Remember that, while you will not be marked down for bad hand-writing, if the examiner cannot read what you have written, then they can't give you the marks you deserve."
>
> Edexcel examiner

The two biggest exam nightmares
Answers by George Turnbull, former examiner

"What if there's a question I just can't answer?"
Don't spend too much time on it. Leave it, attempt other questions, and if you have time left, then go back to that problem question. If you can't remember the answer to a question you know you've studied, just move on, who knows it might just come back to you while you're working on another question.

"What if I run out of time?"
If you've only got 10 minutes left and you've got a 20 or 30-minute question to do? If it's Maths write down the formulae that you would use to solve the problem, saying where you'd get the information from and how you would use it. Add a note saying you ran out of time. That will demonstrate to the examiner that you know how to do the question. If it's an English essay – write down the important details or the main points you would like to make, the main points of your argument, in note/bullet form. Marks can be gained this way because it demonstrates that you know the subject, you just don't have the time to write it out in full.

Recap of PUMP Phase 4: Practise

- Practise is the final piece of your revision puzzle
- Applying what you know solidifies your knowledge and Understanding
- Practising under exam conditions helps battle exam nerves
- It is crucial to get to grips with the Assessment Objectives for each subject
- Past papers are the best way to practise, but you can set up your own practice papers
- Knowledge of keywords, phrases and Understanding of command words gets you marks
- The mark scheme, examiners' reports and sample answers tell you what examiners really want
- Tackle an exam paper calmly and methodically to manage your nerves and your time.

APPLYING PUMP
TO DIFFERENT SUBJECTS

One PUMP fits all

The steps in the PUMP revision approach have been created so they apply to any subject and any level of study. In fact, once you have used PUMP for your GCSEs or A-levels, you are set up to sail through university exam revision as well as any professional exams you might sit later in life. A whole lifetime of learning made easier!

Depending on the subject you are revising you will need to slightly tailor the amount of time you spend on each step and the techniques you select. There are two basic types of exam subjects: content-based and skills-based.

Content-based subjects

These mostly require you to *know* stuff. You need a wide knowledge and an in-depth Understanding of the course content. You need to understand concepts and ideas, as well as little details such as facts, terms or quotations. Content-based subjects include:

Biology

History

Geography

Sociology

Psychology

Economics

Business Studies

Law

Politics

Religious Studies

Skills-based subjects

These mostly require you to *do* stuff. You need to learn tech-niques & methods. There are four different types of skills-based subjects:

A Analyse and evaluate texts or other forms of com-munication	B Solve problems	C Read, write, listen and speak in a foreign language	D Create, design or com-municate
English Language English Literature Philosophy Media studies Film Studies	Maths Physics Chemistry Statistics Accounting Engineering ICT	French German Spanish Hebrew Russian Chinese	Drama/ Theatre Music/Dance Art & Design Photography Design & Technology Home Economics

Of course, many subjects have skills-based and content-based components, requiring you to learn lots of concepts and facts as well as to demonstrate a wide range of skills. The above table is just a rough guide to where subjects largely fall.

There's no doubt that learning how to solve Maths problems or analyse a Shakespeare sonnet is very different from learning Geography topics or the principles of Economics. For skills-based subjects, you need a skills-based approach. The four principles of the PUMP revision approach apply to skills-based and content-based subjects alike. Here's how to tweak the techniques as you switch between skills-based and content-based revision components.

	Content-based subjects	Skills-based subjects
Plan	This applies to all subjects in the same way. Get your hands on the resources you'll need throughout your revision, plan what you're going to revise and when you're going to get down to it.	
Understand	Read your revision resources, using active-reading techniques to build understanding of the concepts and facts.	Refer to the original text or source again and again applying the skills required: for example, study Romeo & Juliet or a French textbook.
	Capture your Understanding in a comprehensive set of Revision Notes without duplications so that you will not have to refer to your Class Notes and textbooks again.	You don't need to make such detailed Revision Notes or paraphrase material. Just make brief notes on the key concepts and terminology e.g., formulae in Maths, German grammar.

	Content-based subjects	Skills-based subjects
Memorise	Condense your notes into Revision Summaries and review regularly to commit to memory.	Condensing into Summaries probably not required. Memorise key facts, rules or quotes from your Revision Notes by testing yourself.
Practise	Once you feel that you know the material, practise exam-style questions to apply what you know.	Spend most revision time on Practice to gain Understanding and memorise. Applying the techniques and facts is the key to learning them.

Of course, the above table is a bit oversimplified but you get the idea. Here's a bit more guidance on how you tailor the PUMP approach for each type of skills-based subject:

A. Analyse and evaluate texts or other form of communication e.g. English Literature

In the Understanding phase of your revision, you'll be reading your texts again and again rather than making and condensing Revision Notes. This is because your job is to analyse *the way the text is written*, not just the ideas presented in the text.

You need to build a solid understanding of each of your texts in detail. You should read each section of your text thoroughly, looking at the main ideas, themes, characters and the author's styles and techniques. You need to create only brief revision notes listing the quotations. Go back to your earlier work and notes and review what your teacher said about this section. As you work through each section of your texts (and then through larger parts of each text) your knowledge and memory will naturally grow. You'll need to actively memorise important quotations to support your answers – use flashcards.

Skills-based subjects demand plenty of Practice. Become familiar with the kind of questions that have been asked in the past, and think about how you might have addressed them.

> "I found I didn't really need to make Revision Notes for English Language and Literature. It merely came down to revising the texts in detail and memorising quotations the night before the exam."
>
> Hannah Bristow, A-grade student

B. Solve problems e.g. Maths

For problem-solving exams like Maths, you need to learn techniques and methods rather than information. You need to understand how to use techniques to solve problems. Reading your textbooks and Class Notes and making Revision Notes will not work. You will build your Understanding of methods and concepts by going through the process of solving problems. So the key is Practice!

There is not much to Memorise (perhaps some formulae that may not be provided in the exam). You mainly need to Memorise the techniques and this comes through Practice.

Solving a range of problems is important as, in the exam you will need to apply your mathematical knowledge to both familiar and unfamiliar problems in both real-world and mathematical contexts. Don't solve the same problems over and over again. Solve new problems. Practise as many problems as possible from your textbook, study guides, online resources etc. and make sure you understand how they were solved. The greater the variety of problems you solve using a given technique, the better you will understand that technique The more problems and the more different types of problems you solve, the better your Understanding will be.

Do it on paper, not in your head. Write down every step. When you get an answer wrong try and work out what went wrong and how you can arrive at the right answer. Keep solving it until you get the right answer.

C. Read, write, listen and speak in a foreign language e.g., French

For foreign languages, you need to demonstrate that you can understand the language (reading and listening) and communicate it (speaking and writing).

As with other skills-based subjects, you don't build Understanding through reading your course materials, writing detailed notes and condensing. Instead, for languages, write brief notes on grammar, vocabulary and key phrases.

- For grammar, write out the rules and examples for each grammar topic e.g., past tense at GCSE, the subjunctive at A-level etc. Practise each grammar point with grammar games and exercises. Practise writing and speaking including each grammar point you have learnt.

- For vocabulary, look at your specification and see what the topic areas are. Make topic-by-topic vocabulary lists. So if health is one of the topics, list all the vocabulary words related to health.

- For the oral exam, write out possible questions and prepare model answers. Test yourself on vocab and oral exam questions/answers until you have Memorised them.

- Read and listen to French as much as possible, read the French press (Le Figaro, Le Monde), listen to French radio (RFI) or watch French TV (TV5).

D. Create, design or communicate

Preparation for these types of exams is out of the scope of this book and not covered by the PUMP approach.

FINAL THOUGHTS

You don't need me to tell you that exams matter. You want some top grades so you can study the subjects you need, get into the university you've set your heart on and ultimately pursue the career of your dreams.

Exam stress

When something is THIS important to you, it's totally normal to feel a fair amount of stress. In fact, if you want to excel yourself, a little pressure can be a good thing.

That little rush of adrenaline you feel in your guts is Mother Nature's best work. It's the 'fight or flight' response to danger, designed to save your life when you're being chased by a sabre-tooth tiger or charged by a woolly mammoth. Nature didn't know about exams back then, but a mammoth makes a good prototype. You run a bit faster, throw your spear a bit harder, you live.

So if a little stress makes you knuckle down, stick to your timetable and get out of bed a bit earlier, all well and good for those A-grades in your sights. But remember that there is no mammoth, no tiger. No risk of being chomped at all. You will get grades, you will live a good life and you will look back and smile.

But if you feel like it's all getting too much, talk to someone about it. Your parents, your teachers or your school counselors can help you deal with stress. Most of the A-grade students I spoke to did feel stressed during revision; they mentioned the importance of sleeping well, eating well, exercise and positive thinking. All good advice.

Stress management tips

"Get enough sleep! Everything seems a million times worse if you're overtired. You realise your life probably isn't over if you mess up an exam after you've had a decent night's sleep."
Laura Bates, A-Grade student

"It's important not to isolate yourself completely and lock yourself up in your room, you need a certain amount of time with your friends and family every day to give you perspective and take you out of your revision bubble".
Megan Powell, A-Grade student Highlight

"I found writing checklists therapeutic as I could tick off what I had done each day which gave me confidence that I had achieved something, and that I deserved a break!"
Emily Motto, A-Grade student

"I think the most important thing is to stick to a plan and keeping to a sensible daily routine. I don't revise in the hour or so before I go to bed, otherwise I can't sleep properly. Also socialising during exams tends to just make me nervous, and I've learnt it's best to avoid particularly competitive friends during exam time or walk away when the conversation turns towards revision."
Daisy Gibbs, A-Grade student

"Make your parents set a limit if you're an overworker: they should force you to go on a day out with them every now and then if they see you driving yourself crazy."

Morganne Graves, A-Grade student

"I think that a change of atmosphere is also always beneficial in helping to reduce stress. If I got stressed out, I'd take a break, then move to a different room. It is kind of like moving away from the 'stressful' area or negative atmosphere, you feel much fresher and ready to work again. I think it is important to know, before the whole revision process though, that revising is like a marathon and that there are so many points when you kind of feel like just giving up."

Rita Teo, A-Grade student

More stress management tips

"Going for a run, or some form of exercise relaxes your eyes as well as your mind."

Elizabeth Roe, A-Grade student

"They are just exams. They will always be just that. Treat it as a challenge: they are something to conquer, not be terrified of."

Thomas Pollard, A-Grade student

"Have 3 decent meals a day. Always have good breakfast to keep you going and get you out of bed. Doing instrumental practice was good stress relief."

Tom Nichols, A-Grade student

Procrastination

We all do this from time to time but some people are professional procrastinators. If you have a strong streak of the 'put-it-off-until-laters', rest assured, revision will bring it out, like Vanish brings out Ribena stains. When you procrastinate, you actively look for distractions: you check your email, you loiter around on Facebook, you make another snack, you redo your revision timetable for the gazillionth time. The more pressure you are under, the more your procrastination gremlins do their thing. Long-beards think procrastination is either a way of avoiding responsibility, controlling the fear of failure or seeking thrills. Anyone fancy the euphoric rush of panic? Either way, it's not good for you – or your grades. Come revision time, procrastination is an official time-sapping evil and it will drain your super powers. Try these tips from A-grade achievers, who managed to put their procrastination off until after exams.

Procrastination-busters

"For each subject I had a set amount of things I wanted to get done before the exam. For example, go over the 6 topics, and then do 10 practise papers. It was also motivational in that it was not a time constraint but an 'output' or 'achievement' constraint. So procrastination was a waste of my time and completely useless, since I knew that I would have to complete the tasks that day."

Morganne Graves, A-Grade student

"I found it helpful to keep my 'procrastination' activities separate (physically) from where I work. This meant that I would have to walk through the house all the way to my bedroom before I could procrastinate which meant I could stop myself!".

Rita Teo, A-Grade Student

"If I was procrastinating I would write myself a note laying out the aims of my life e.g. I want to go to uni to study etc. and earn enough to buy myself such and such a car, and to do this I must do well in these exams."

Miriam Steinmann, A-Grade student

More procrastination-busters

"I got someone to change my FB password so I couldn't use it during exams."

Elizabeth Roe, A-Grade student

"The best way of avoiding it would be to wake up and immediately start revising, before even showering and having breakfast because I've then set up the day to be one of revision."

Megan Powell, A-Grade student

Even more procrastination-busters

"I found "going to make tea" was a massive procrastination process, as was snacking. I rationed myself to one Facebook login a day, and in some cases banned myself from it entirely."

Hannah Bristow, A-Grade student

"I would revise in my local library and coffee shop where there were no distractions! In those places I felt more pressure to work in case anyone was watching (as I was surrounded by others) whereas in my room or around the house at home I would feel less self conscious so could easily while my time away doing something irrelevant."

Emily Motto, A-Grade student

"I told my parents and siblings if they saw more procrastinating, to mention revision which would stop me from procrastinating further."

Susie Archer, A-Grade student

13894165R00081

Printed in Great Britain
by Amazon.co.uk, Ltd.,
Marston Gate.